Your Real Estate Closing Explained Simply

What Smart Buyers & Sellers Need to Know

By
Michelle Blain

Your Real Estate Closing Explained Simply
What Smart Buyers & Sellers Need To Know

ISBN-13: 978-1-60138-032-6 • ISBN-10: 1-60138-032-1

Library of Congress Cataloging-in-Publication Data
Blain, Michelle, 1974-
   Your real estate closing explained simply : what smart buyers & sellers need to know / by Michelle Blain.
       p. cm.
   Includes bibliographical references and index.
   ISBN-13: 978-1-60138-032-6 (alk. paper)
   ISBN-10: 1-60138-032-1 (alk. paper)
   1. Settlement costs--United States. 2. Mortgage loans--Law and legislation--United States. 3. Vendors and purchasers--United States. I. Title.

   KF681.B53 2007
   346.7304'373--dc22
                                        2006038842
   2006034245

Printed on Recycled Paper

Printed in the United States

Table of Contents

Contents

Dedication & Biography

This book is dedicated to those embarking on the American Dream journey. May you get your wishes. Also to my husband, Shawn Miller, thank you for your support.

Born and raised in Carlisle, Pennsylvania, Michelle Blain studied English Literature and Education at Le Moyne College in Syracuse, New York. While in New York, she worked in the public school system as a reading and grammar tutor. She later graduated from the University of Arizona with a BA in English and Business Administration. She currently lives in Tucson, Arizona, where she works as a freelance writer for various businesses and publications.

She became interested in real estate while maneuvering the maze of her first home purchase. After which, she realized the need for a comprehensive guide, and wrote this book, a compilation of research and advice from professionals, at the suggestion and through the generous support of Atlantic Publishing.

Author

Acknowledgements

Through the generous contributions of top professionals and everyday people, this book will guide your understanding of the basics of real estate, the various players, their responsibilities to you and each other, and the documents they will present to you. Thank you to the following individuals and organizations:

Eric T. Magoon, Esquire
Law Offices of Eric T. Magoon
1031 Ives Dairy Road, Suite 228
North Miami Beach, Florida
T: 305-914-3765 / F: 305-914-0158
E-Mail: eric@erictmagoon.com

Noelle Matzek
Recent Home Buyer

Terry and Roger Blain
Rental Property Owners

Chris Florko
Recent Home Buyer

Geneva Jones
Benchmark Mortgage, Inc
3990 SW Collins Way #202
Lake Oswego, OR 97035

Eric Bozinny
Agent, Consultant, Investor
Seattle, Washington
Visit his blog at
http://seattlerei.blogspot.com

Nancy Spivey
Coach and Speaker
Transformation Consultants, Inc.
P.O. Box 190075
Atlanta, GA 31119
T: 770-377-1847
http://www.transformit.net

Fred Ugast of Home Tech
for granting copyright privileges
for the home inspection forms
http://www.hometechonline.com

Foreword

Foreword

Many people dream of owning a home or business property, but not so many actually make the leap. If you are considering home ownership for the first or the tenth time, become familiar or update your experience by becoming aware of the requirements of having a successful closing. That information is what this book is all about: getting you through closing efficiently and without undue costs. If "fear of closing" is holding you back, remember that real estate ownership has historically yielded high returns.

By reading this book, because it is more than just a typical "how to" guide, you will be prepared to glide through a process that can trip up even professionals. This is a comprehensive guide that explains the basic concepts in easy-to-understand terms, showing you concrete ways you can buy and sell smoothly. For the seasoned buyer, there are tips and ideas for saving yourself many a headache from the unexpected.

The difference between this book and others is that this book focuses on really doing a real estate deal correctly. You must have a solid understanding of the business and good practices to be a success. By following the map that has been laid out, anyone will be able to create real estate closing success.

If you are facing a real estate deal and are wondering what the closing costs consist of and how to reduce them, what are points, when do you need prepaid homeowner's insurance, how much is an appraisal fee, lawyer's fee, recording fee, title search and insurance, how to calculate tax adjustments, agent commissions, and mortgage insurance, this is the book for you.

The research stage of buying real estate takes time, but it could mean the difference between making or losing money, so make time for it. Once you are ready, you will move from research to buying. It will undoubtedly be an exciting time.

Eric T. Magoon, Esquire
Law Offices of Eric T. Magoon
1031 Ives Dairy Road, Suite 228
North Miami Beach, Florida
Telephone: 305-914-3765
Fax: 305-914-0158
E-mail: eric@erictmagoon.com

Introduction

When most people imagine a real estate deal, they think about being handed the keys or the check. In reality, the deal begins with the purchase offer and moves through a defined process that could last several months. After a purchase offer has been made, the days become intense as parties assess counter offers, disclosures, lease agreements, surveys, inspections, and mortgage options to name a few of the steps involved. Not surprisingly, anyone with real estate experience will advise taking the time to form a basic understanding of real estate transactions and securing trustworthy, experienced representation before initiating a deal.

For many individuals, the buying or selling of a property is one of the most important events of their life because, as everyone hopes, it represents a substantial economic gain. Because so much is at stake, buyers and sellers should understand the process. Of course, every real estate transaction is unique and will present challenges of its own. However, a basic understanding of the buying and selling process is an important tool for maneuvering those challenges.

We experienced a tumultuous time in the housing market between early 2004 and late 2005 because of unprecedented low interest rates. Many people made a profit, many lost their shirts, and others just ended up staying in houses for longer than they expected. Now we find ourselves in a new era of reasonableness. This book addresses the new market by guiding buyers and sellers with sound, practical advice. As Benjamin Franklin said, "A penny of prevention is worth a pound of cure."

chapter one

Preliminary Matters

My sister put the plates down next to the vase as she scolded her son, telling him to hold the teacups with both hands. I stood in the dining room, wrapping dinner plates in newspaper, watching the commotion as she waded through boxes to answer the teakettle. This was the last day we would live in an apartment with brown carpet and white walls. We were going to our new house. I woke up that night to look at the walls for the last time, saying goodbye, thinking, I am going to my place, feeling joy in every cell as I whispered it to myself in the dark.

Every year more than 1.4 million people by their first home. Opportunities to make your financial dreams come true are there, and this book will guide you systematically from the beginning of a real estate transaction to the end. We begin with the typical first order of business, selecting a real estate agent.

Section 1.01: What Is a Real Estate Agent?

A buyer or seller should be acting under the guidance of an individual who has been independently licensed by the state to sell real estate. Licenses are never shared within a business. Typically, agents must obtain a preliminary license and work under another agent for several years as a sales person before becoming an independent agent. This means you may work with a person who has not been fully licensed, but that individual's work must be supervised by a fully licensed agent. The licensing process is not federally regulated and varies from state to state although every state has a regulatory agency that issues licenses. Check with your state's representative agency for specific licensing criteria and the credentials required to obtain licensing. Each state agency maintains a public list of agents in good standing sometimes online.

Of course, the agent's job is to find a property for a buyer or to find a buyer for a seller. This seems deceptively simple. If the agent is working for the buyer, he or she must comb through listings searching for properties that match the buyer's criteria. If the market is hot, this could be a huge job. The agent must understand how to value property to ensure the real estate is worth the listed price. A good agent will visit properties ahead of the buyer to look for obvious problems that might eliminate that property from consideration. He or she will understand the market in different areas of a city or state and know if a property is likely to appreciate or depreciate, guiding the buyer. Agents represent their clients during the negotiation process. Some buyers choose to have their agent make the purchase contract and some hire an attorney. An agent should have a general understanding of real estate law and be able to draw up the purchase contract.

If the agent is working for the seller, he or she lists the property prominently to attract buyers, knows the market, and gives advice. The agent will schedule, advertise, attend, and guide the seller through open houses. They lead the negotiation process, serving as the primary contact for potential buyers.

Agents always charge a commission fee after the real estate transaction has been completed, but should not charge a fee just for giving advice or for retaining their services. If you are asked to pay any up front fees, you should find another agent. Real estate commissions are usually six percent for a developed property and 10 percent for raw land, paid by the seller after closing. FHA and Fannie Mae have their own commission requirements that are different from market standards. Typically, the buyer's agent will be paid out of this six percent commission, but commission fee requirements should be made clear and agreed to in writing up front. I cannot emphasize this enough. If the agent refuses to disclose the fee, find out what the commission will be, compare that to the going rate, and decide whether to go with another agent.

When choosing a real estate agent, take a number of things into consideration. Of course, the fees must be considered. Also, think about the reputation of the agency: ask your friends, relatives, and coworkers for recommendations. Find out how much experience your agent has and the age of the agency. You will probably visit your agent's office numerous times. Pick one that is close to your house if it is possible.

There is one last thing buyers and sellers should understand about real estate agents. An agent has a fiduciary relationship with his or her client. The nature of this legal relationship is commonly misunderstood. It means all information that is passed between the agent and the client is to be held in confidence. It also means each party's respective agent has a duty to get the best possible deal for said client. However, lying, cheating, withholding information that could financially damage other parties, or otherwise committing fraud is not permissible. An agent who participates in these activities can be fined, suffer a license suspension or loss, and in the most serious cases be imprisoned for fraud. If you believe an agent has acted fraudulently or that problems with a property are being purposely withheld, you should report this behavior to your state licensing bureau.

> **TIP**
>
> Always get a commission statement before working with an agent. Under certain circumstances, commission fees will be required even if the property does not sell. For example, if a buyer fails to secure financing before closing, commission fees may be due to the agent. You want to be clear about these details. Buyers and sellers should understand that a commission statement is legally binding.

Section 1.02: Should You Hire an Attorney?

There are many reasons buyers and sellers may want to hire an attorney before closing. The main consideration is obvious: retaining legal expertise. An attorney can explain the legal terms of documents such as prepayment, penalties, and points. For example, a buyer may not realize the mortgage contract has a prepayment penalty, requiring the payment of six months of interest should the loan be paid off within two years or that the mortgage agent is charging 2 points or 2 percent of the loan amount and an administrative fee.

Many people are involved in the closing process, including real estate agents, surveyors, home inspectors, mortgage agents, and title insurance underwriters. An attorney can keep the process organized and moving toward closing on time.

Should a conflict arise, an attorney who already has an understanding of your closing will be at your service with advice and representation.

Section 1.03: The Seller's Perspective

Valuation

Determining the value of a property is one of the seller's most important tasks. Property should not be undervalued for obvious reasons, but overvalued property will not sell. If it sits on the market for too long, buyers will offer less, assuming you are desperate to sell. The following is the basic valuation process.

- Locate several other properties in the same general area that have similar characteristics such as age, type of construction, and amenities.

- Find the most recent selling price of these properties.

- Divide the most recent selling price of each property by its square footage.

- Find the average.

- Apply this average square foot price to your property.

Case Study: Eric T. Magoon

Entering into a real estate contract is one of the most important financial decisions a person will make in life and it is wise to seek counsel. Here is an example of how an attorney can help. The buyer enters into a $1 million contract. He deposits $100,000. The closing date is set for 30 days. The  attorney would advise the buyer he must close within 30 days or forfeit the deposit. If he does not think he can close in that time, the attorney can possibly negotiate an extension of the closing date and draft an addendum to the contract. Without the attorney's advice, the buyer may read over the closing date terms, not understand the significance, and fail to be prepared for the closing. Result: the buyer would forfeit a $100,000 deposit. The attorney also helps to ensure that the terms of the documents are enforced. For instance, he or she will make sure the buyer obtains the new loan commitment within the specified period.

Every property will have other factors to take into consideration aside from a straightforward valuation. For example, the market may have gone up dramatically in the last few months, you may be in a strong buyers' market, or you may need to sell quickly for personal reasons. An experienced real estate agent can be a good source of advice when considering factors outside of the valuation.

Seller's Inspections Prior to Listing

Sellers should have building and termite/pest inspections done before putting a property on the market because they want to know about potential hidden problems and correct them in advance on their terms. Almost all purchase offers include the condition that the contract is contingent on completion of satisfactory inspections. Most buyers will insist that the inspection be a professional home inspection, usually by an inspector they hire. If the buyer's inspector finds a problem, it could cause the deal to fall through. At best, surprise problems uncovered by the buyer's inspector will cause the closing to be delayed, and you will have to pay for repairs at the last minute or take a lower price for your property.

Another point to keep in mind regarding the buyer's inspectors: their inspectors will not only inspect the property, but will also stand to make a sum of money if you agree to do his or her suggested repairs. Therefore, these individuals' best interests are served by finding necessary repairs and recommending the most expensive solution. You will want to have you own inspection reports and estimates to use as negotiating tools if the buyer presents an outlandish estimate during escrow. Choose a company that has a solid reputation even if you need to wait for an appointment. You should plan to be present for your inspection. Have every problem explained to you in detail and ask for every repair alternative to be put in writing.

Does the Seller Have to Repair Everything?

The seller's inspection report is not intended to be a repair list. Sellers are not obligated to repair conditions noted in the report, nor are they required to produce a flawless house. With a pre-listing home inspection, potential repair items already known by both parties are subject to negotiations. A home seller can make repairs as a matter of choice, not obligation, to foster good will or to facilitate the sale. Sellers maintain the right to refuse repair demands, except where required by state law, local ordinances, or the real estate purchase contract.

Should You Hire a Real Estate Agent?

Every seller asks, "Should I hire an agent or handle this myself?" Of course, the seller typically pays most of the commission fees, but there are trade offs for not paying for the services of an agent. You will not have access to the advice of an experienced person and you have to do all the work. Here are a few duties you will have to take over without an agent.

- List, advertise, and host your own open house.

- Speak with every potential buyer, answering every question yourself.

- Give a tour to every potential buyer.

- Value your own property and negotiate a selling price on your own behalf.

- Review the purchase offers yourself or hire an attorney to read them for you.

This work is time-consuming and interrupts your personal and work life. Also consider your personal attachment to the property. Can you be removed and realistic about the price during the negotiation process. Many people self-sell and do a fantastic job, but not everyone can be detached enough to think of their home as a business deal. Just be aware of what you will be getting into before you decide to self-sell. Here is a "Seller's Flowchart" with the selling process from start to finish.

SELLER'S FLOWCHART

#1	Physically prepare the house to be shown	↓
#2	Choose a real estate broker	Choose a real estate attorney
#3	Have the property's value assessed	Have the title researched if it is in question, clear the title
#4	List the property	↓
#5	Negotiate a price with the representation of a RE broker	↓
#6	↓	Attorney prepares some closing documents such as estoppel letters, reviews closing documents
#7	Receives a commission fee	Provides representation during the closing, Arranges the payment of fees

OPEN HOUSE CHECKLIST

TASKS TO DO WHEN PREPARING FOR AN OPEN HOUSE	TASKS TO DO IMMEDIATELY BEFORE AN OPEN HOUSE
• Survey the house for necessary repairs. • Repair holes in the walls. • Replace old or dulled pain. • Clean or replace stained or soiled carpeting. • Clean dusty window coverings and furnishings. • Discard, donate, or sell unwanted items stored that create clutter. • Clean thoroughly. • Arrange for a babysitter.	• Heat or cool the building as needed. • Pick up and put away clutter. • Put the toilet seats down. • Close the shower curtains. • Remove used towels. • Air out the house. • Take out the trash • Make sure the buyers have adequate parking

Section 1.04: The Buyer's Perspective

What are Mortgages, Deeds of Trust, and Promissory Notes?

In most cases, the buyer's lender will lend against the property that is being purchased, which means the property itself is the collateral for the loan, and the lender draws up a Deed of Trust. In some states, it is called a Mortgage Deed. These documents describe the property and give the lender the legal right to foreclose and sell the property to get the money owed if the loan is not repaid. The borrower will be asked to sign a promissory note, a legally binding IOU that must state the amount owed and the date due. Once the borrower has signed a promissory note that is backed up by a Deed of Trust, they become the *trustor*. In states that use a Mortgage Deed this person is called the *mortgagor*. The lender becomes the *beneficiary* or the entity that is owed or the *trustee* or the holder of the Deed of Trust.

There are two types of promissory notes, straight and installment. Payments to a straight note are only applied to the interest due. When the note is due, the principal must be paid in full. This type of note is usually set up for a construction loan which the borrower intends to refinance or sell after construction has been completed. Installment notes are set up according to a payment schedule. Each time a payment is received some part is applied to interest and the rest is applied to the principal.

THE BORROWER'S BILL OF RIGHTS

A Borrower has the right to mortgage loans that show benefit to the borrower and his or her circumstances.

A Borrower has the right to a clear, understandable explanation of the terms, conditions, and costs of his or her loan.

A Borrower has the right to receive his or her credit score rating and top reasons for these scores from each reporting agency.

A Borrower has the right to inquire and receive accurate and up-to-date information regarding the status of his or her loan.

A Borrower has the right to timely, truthful disclosures regarding his or her loan.

A Borrower has the right to a copy of his or her appraisal.

A Borrower has the right to choose his or her title and escrow service.

A Borrower has the right to be given the facts about credit life insurance and has the right to use or not to use this service. A Borrower has the right to choose whether taxes and insurance will be paid monthly from an escrow account, or individually as they may present themselves.

The Borrower has the right to be educated as to the benefits of each choice.

This information provided by and reprinted with the permission of:
Geneva Jones of
Benchmark Mortgage, Inc
"The Standard By Which Others Are Measured"
3990 SW Collins Way #202
Lake Oswego, OR 97035

Because a mortgage is a significant legal and financial commitment, buyers should have a clear understanding of it. There are real estate mortgages and commercial mortgages. The difference is determined by the type of property being used for collateral. Additionally, commercial mortgages are usually made on behalf of a company and not an individual with the lender unable to seize any property other than that used as collateral in the event of a foreclosure. The legal term for this is no recourse. Due to this, commercial mortgages are usually underwritten based entirely on the attributes of the property being mortgaged, as opposed to the credit attributes of the borrower as is the case with real estate mortgages. Within the scope of this book, to underwrite is to perform a detailed credit analysis. However, underwriting can also mean the purchase of corporate bonds, commercial paper, government securities, municipal general obligation bonds by a commercial bank or dealer bank for its own account or for resale to investors.

A mortgage encompasses more than just a repayment of the money borrowed to purchase a property. Because the lender has lent against the property, the lender has a stake in it. Therefore, the lender will set up stipulations regarding what types of protective insurances must be carried. Usually this will be at least fire insurance and a general homeowner's policy. If the property is in a flood plane, flood insurance will also be required. The premiums for these policies will be collected monthly along with the loan payment. The lender will also maintain copies of the borrower's insurance certificates, the written promise of insurance from the insurance carrier. A property can be foreclosed by governmental agencies in the event the property taxes are not paid. To ensure this does not happen, the yearly tax owed will be broken into monthly payments and collected with the monthly loan payments, creating the last portion of the mortgage payment.

Where Can a Buyer Get Financing?

Financing can be obtained from many places, including the seller. Non-traditional financing will be discussed in Chapter 6, while this section will only discuss the basics. Borrowers have four main choices: credit unions, savings and loans, mortgage brokers, or banks (mortgage bankers). Credit unions are like private banks in that they are based on a cooperative banking model developed in 19th-century Europe. People pool their money and make loans to each other. The guiding principles have remained the same to the present. Only people who are credit union members can borrow. Loans are made for productive purposes only, to make money for depositors. Last, an individual's desire to repay and character are more important than the person's ability to repay or income. After all, members are borrowing their own money and that of their friends. These principles still govern most of the world's credit unions. The difference between a savings and loan and a credit union basically is that a credit union is a not-for-profit cooperative institution that is owned and controlled by its members, through a Board of Directors elected from the membership. Only a member of a credit union may deposit money with the credit union or borrow money from it. A savings and loan may be publicly owned and traded. The depositors may or may not have managerial control. It is always operated for profit.

> **TIP**
>
> Credit unions sometimes give outstanding interest rates to attract business and to compete with public banks. Because good credit is given precedent over income, and low income does not automatically mean a higher interest rate will be given; middle and lower income people may be able to get a good deal at a credit union. The downside is usually certain criteria must be met to become a member. For example, the credit union might be for state employees only or for members of certain unions. You should check the admittance policies of your local credit unions as you might meet them. Joining could be to your benefit.

What is a Mortgage Broker? What is a Mortgage Banker?

The mortgage broker/banker's primary duties are to meet with the borrower and find out what the borrower intends to do with the property and to ascertain the borrower's financial situation. After initial information is gathered, the broker or banker can assess which loan program and interest rate will be the best fit. The broker/banker should guide the buyer to make the best financial decision, lock in an interest rate to protect the borrower, satisfy all the conditions of the loan, ensure the appropriate documents are completed and returned on time, and work with the attorney or title agent to close on the property. The broker/ banker must ensure that the loan is processed and secured in time for the borrower to close on the scheduled date and can attend the closing to answer questions if the borrower wishes.

As the previous paragraph indicates, primarily the broker and banker have the same responsibilities. However, a mortgage banker is a direct employee of the bank from which the borrower intends to borrow. A mortgage broker works through a private company. There are downsides to both options. The bank employee may give the borrower access to borrowing incentives, special deals a bank will offer to encourage its customers to borrow, but he or she is working for the bank — not you. Anyone can see how this situation may not always lend itself to being in the borrower's best interest. On the other hand, a private mortgage broker is employed by the borrower so the broker's best interest is served by doing what is best for the borrower, like locking in an interest rate at the most opportune time. Unfortunately, the private broker may not be able to offer the borrower the same bank sponsored incentives. What does this mean? Borrowers should shop around.

What is Prequalification and Why is it Important?

To be prequalified means you have submitted personal financial information to a lender who decided you would be a good loan candidate. This lender will give a *commitment letter* to you and any parties requesting it with your approval. The letter shows that you are a qualified buyer but does not guarantee a loan or any loan terms. This commitment letter will allow you to make decisions quickly when you begin shopping for a property and will be especially helpful during the negotiation process, as it will indicate your financial boundaries. Most lenders will not charge for a commitment letter. Therefore, getting one as part of your shopping process will serve you well. Another point to consider, as discussed earlier, many real estate agents require a commission fee payment even if the property does not sell because the borrower failed to secure financing before closing. Even though the seller is primarily responsible for the payment of commission fees, not coming through with financing could leave you open to legal problems. Why take this chance when you can get prequalified for free?

Case Study: Eric Bozinny

This anecdote demonstrates how real estate opportunities can present themselves quickly. Buyers must have prequalification to know their financial reach before they begin working with an agent.

Recently when I was in Miami, I received an e-mail from our agent who often comes across investment opportunities and sends e-mails out to her list of investors to see who responds most quickly—first come, first serve. Being in Miami, I overlooked this e-mail. I forwarded it to my wife, and she was able to look into the details.

Because the sellers want to sell quietly, our agent invited all interested parties to meet at her office to review the property. My wife and I were worried because there were two other interested investors on the tour with us. After the 30-minute tour of the home and land, our agent asked who wanted to write up an offer. Immediately, my wife said "We do." Fortunately, the other investors were not interested. I was surprised. It turns out that these others have only done much smaller deals and thought this one was beyond their reach financially. Our gain.

What are Some Additional Reasons to Get Prequalification?

After a property has been chosen, the potential buyer will give a purchase offer to the seller. Earnest money will be given with the offer. This money is given as a sign of good faith that the buyer's offer is serious. If the deal falls through because the buyer could not secure financing, the earnest money is forfeited. In addition, the buyer traditionally pays the inspection, survey, and appraisal fees that will also be forfeited without financing prior to closing.

Escrows proceed quickly. The buyer is expected to schedule and be present for inspections and surveys and for the repairs that are discovered during the inspection process, make utility transfer arrangements, read lengthy legal documents, and make moving arrangements. Your home financing is one of the most important decisions you will make in your life. You would be best served by making these arrangements before escrow when your attention is on many other things. Consider this; every .05 percent of interest represents $30 to $40 per month, an excellent reason to take the time to shop around.

Loan Shopping Tips

- Compare loan fees. They are important because they are substantial. Loan fees are discussed in detail later in this section.

- Find the interest rate being offered by each lender.

- Ask if you can lock in an interest rate because the escrow process takes several weeks.

- Find out what types of loans are available to you.

| TIP | Some lenders will give a lump-sum payment to new borrowers at the beginning of a mortgage, called cash back. This lump sum is often marketed as free cash, but it is in fact rolled into the mortgage. Cash back is popular with first time buyers who usually put it toward moving-related expenses. |

- The Internet can facilitate loan shopping. Many sites will give an answer within minutes. Only use sites that begin with https. The "s" stands for secure.

How Much Can Be Borrowed?

A traditional home loan lender will typically grant up to 80 percent of the value of the property. However, some lenders will go up to 90 percent. Lenders will usually grant up to 70 percent of a commercial property's value. As a reflection of the real estate market's recent performance, lenders have begun offering 100 percent loans. This is usually done by borrowing 20 percent of the total cost as a home equity line of credit.

Lenders will decide how much you qualify to borrow by getting your FICO score from one of the major credit bureaus. Certain factors such as pre-existing outstanding debt, previous failure to pay on debts and routinely unpaid utility bills are used to determine the score. The scores can range from 300 to 900, with the average American scoring around 700. You can find your score at **www.myfico.com**.

If your score is low, you can improve it by paying down debt, eliminating some revolving accounts, and paying your bills on time. You should know your score will lower every time your credit report is requested. Therefore, you should limit the number of times you request credit. Many nonprofit credit repair agencies can help you to get back on track for free or for a very small fee, although having them do so will lower your score by 100 points.

Calculating Amortization

To calculate amortization means to find the exact dollar amount that will go toward interest and the exact dollar amount that will go toward principal out of each individual monthly payment of a mortgage. Borrowers should have an understanding of this to control their financial futures. A brief search will lead to any number of Web sites that offer free amortization calculators. You will simply need to know what your maximum monthly payment amount is. Then run the amortization calculation backwards to determine how much principal you can afford to borrow. However, remember that a basic amortization calculator will only account for the cost of repaying the interest and principal of a loan. Other costs involved with home ownership such as taxes, insurances, and Homeowner's Association fees will lower the amount of money you have available. These calculators can also be run backwards to find the payoffs on investments.

The compound interest amortization formula follows.

$$A = \frac{P\,i\,(1+i)^n}{(1+i)^n - 1}$$

A = periodic payment amount
P = amount of principal
i = periodic interest rate
n = total number of payments
    (for a 30-year loan with monthly
    payments, n = 30 years × 12
    months = 360)

What is an Affordability Analysis?

A responsible mortgage broker will request an affordability analysis or at least provide one for the borrower to complete privately. This analysis will help the buyer determine how much they can spend on a monthly mortgage in concrete terms. An affordability analysis is a great tool. One has been included at the end of this chapter in the form of a monthly expenses worksheet.

> **TIP**
>
> During the first third of your loan term, each month most of your loan payment will be applied directly to interest. The following month your interest due is calculated by the amount of remaining principal. Lenders maximize their profits by arranging loans in this way. If you can choose between a 15-year mortgage and a 30-year mortgage, choose the 30-year mortgage. A 30-year mortgage will offer lower monthly payments. Any extra money sent with the monthly payment will be applied directly to the principal, slightly lowering your monthly interest due the following month. This effect will compound month after month creating a substantial interest savings for the borrower and still allowing for repayment in 15 years.

Other Housing Affordability Measurements

Other affordability measurements, used by economists, could be helpful to you. For example, if you are thinking of moving to a certain neighborhood in a new city, the *price to income ratio* will present information about the standard of living as it is affected by housing prices. Basically, the *price to income ratio* is the housing affordability measurement in a given area. It is the average house price compared to the average familial disposable income, expressed as a percentage. It is sometimes called attainability. This percentage will tell you how much money you are likely to have left after making your mortgage payment if you are living and working in a certain location. Of course, this is based on the established premise that your disposable income directly correlates to your standard of living.

The *deposit to income ratio* is the minimum required down payment for a typical mortgage, expressed in months or years of income. It is especially important for first-time buyers without existing home equity because if the down payment becomes too high, some buyers will be priced out of the market. A rising deposit-to-income ratio typically indicates economy will soon experience a buyers' market or more sellers than buyers. It acts as a tip to consumers because obviously buyers want to purchase in a buyers' market if they are not priced out, and sellers should avoid selling in a buyers' market. A variant of this ratio measures the average family income to the income needed to qualify for a mortgage.

The *median home price* divides the real estate market into two equal halves; one-half is above the median and the other is below. Finding the median home price for a certain area will indicate if you can realistically expect to find a property in your price range. It is the most common measurements used to compare real estate prices in different markets, areas, and periods. It is more reliable than just finding the average (the mean home price) since it is not as heavily influenced by the top 2 percent of homes in the area. The median history will indicate the stability of the market in a specific area. Because real estate adjusts with inflation, investors frequently use it to shield money. Investors interested in sheltering their money from inflation by purchasing real estate should research the median.

Other Affordability Factors to Consider

Rising home prices can be caused by urban renewal. The rising home prices themselves can initiate a cycle in which the rising prices fuel the renewal and vice versa, transforming unprofitable and decaying properties into gold mines. Many downtown areas of large cities are currently enjoying a reawakening of interest, creating opportunities for investors and for lower-income first-time home buyers.

Before buying in that cheap new housing development, consider that real estate prices will drop with low demand and a surplus in supply. This trend is largely motivated by an overestimation of suburban migration in which developers buy inexpensive raw land, develop it, and sell it cheap with the promise that its value will increase due to additional planned development. The property value will increase only if demand holds out. Otherwise, the value will drop. Investors should form an understanding of the market in surrounding communities as well as price discrimination.

Price discrimination is an economic principle that describes how a market will capture consumer surplus. First, understand a surplus arises because in a market with a consistent price some consumers would be prepared to pay more than this single market price and some less. Price discrimination transfers some of this surplus from the consumer to the seller. For example, some sellers will get top dollar, but as the surplus increases above the number of consumers, sellers are forced to charge less and less to capture the remaining segment of consumers who are not willing to pay as much as the original purchasers. If you sell in a surplus market, you may be forced to lower your price until you find a buyer. Obviously, this is not in the favor of an investor.

Due to rising oil prices, some lenders are offering "location efficient mortgages" which are available to people who buy in locations where cars are not required. With traditional mortgages, there is a monthly payment cut-off based on the borrower's income to ensure that after the mortgage is granted, the household will have the ability to pay for all other obligations. Location-efficient mortgages allow borrowers to own more expensive homes than they normally would be able to own by adding the money they will save on transportation costs into the allowable monthly mortgage payment, creating a win-win situation for the borrower and the environment.

Commercial investors should seriously consider the payback period or the length of time required for the cash flow from a project to equal the amount of money invested. A lack of cash flow is the main cause of business bankruptcy in the United States.

Which Ongoing Home Ownership Costs Should Be Taken Into Consideration?

When considering a home purchase, assume every appliance will need to be replaced at some point. Assume the roof, heater, cooling system, landscaping, sidewalks will all need to be replaced eventually. Until a property has been decided upon and the inspections have been completed, you will not have more than a general idea regarding your home maintenance expenses. However, a good rule is to keep enough money on hand to make the most expensive possible repair. In all likelihood, this will be the furnace, the cooling system, or a major roof repair. When calculating your maximum monthly mortgage payment, allow a cushion to go into savings for this.

What Fees Will Be Charged During the Lending Process?

Buyers who intend to get a mortgage should consider lender fees that can be substantial and can decrease funds available for a down payment, ultimately affecting the monthly mortgage payment. Because fees vary from lender to lender, you should get them up front. The lender is required by the Truth in Lending Act to reveal all the fees to you. The lender's fees will appear on the closing statement, but the time to find out about fees is not during closing.

The following is a list of typical loan fees.

- **Loan Origination Fee*** — the fee charged by the lender for lending the money.

- **Buy Down Fee** — Some lenders will allow the borrower to "buy down" the interest rate (points).

- **Appraisal Fee*** — The lender will have the property's value assessed before issuing a Deed of Trust. The borrower pays for this service.

- **Credit Report Fee*** — The borrower must reimburse the lender for the fee paid to get the borrower's credit report.

- **Inspection Fee*** — Most lenders will conduct their own inspection to ensure the property is everything the borrower claimed it to be. This is different from a home inspection and should not take the place of a home inspection.

- **Tax Servicing Fee** — A fee charged to a borrower by a lender so that another company will assume responsibility for verifying the amount of real estate taxes due.

- **Processing Fee*** — Fee charged by the lender for moving money to facilitate the loan.

- **Mortgage Broker Fee** — The borrower must pay the mortgage broker a commission.

- **Broker Origination Fee** — The borrower must pay the broker a fee for finding a lender.

- **Application Fee** — The lender's fee for processing the borrower's loan application.

- **Administrative Fee/Document Preparation Fee** — The lender's fee for processing the loan documents.

- **Underwriting Fee** — A fee charged by some lenders to cover the cost of the lender's analysis of the risk associated with a loan.

- **Down Payment** — The buyer's down payment is collected at the closing but is agreed upon in advance when the terms of the loan are worked out.

* These fees are usually negotiable.

These fees are directly tied to the loan. Additional fees are paid at closing, including a settlement or closing fee paid to the title agent or real estate attorney and a fee for the issuance of title insurance,. A buyer should expect to pay at least $3,000 in fees upon purchasing a $150,000 property. The fees will increase proportionate to the cost of the property.

What Are Points?

A point is sometimes called an origination fee or a discount point and is a fee for establishing a new loan. It is also one of the factors used in calculating the annual percentage rate. It is a charge assessed by a lending institution to increase the yield of a mortgage loan to make it meet the current market rate and to be competitive with other investments. One point represents 1 percent of the loan amount. The fee usually varies from ½ percent or ½ a point to 2 percent or two points of the total loan amount. Some lenders will charge points plus an origination fee. If a $100,000 loan carries 1-½ percentage points, the borrower will pay $1,500 at closing. The loan interest rate is calculated by beginning with a standard rate such as the federal interest rate and adding the applicable points. Borrowers should keep in mind that points may be negotiable and can sometimes be bought down when the loan is originated.

What is a Yield Spread Fee?

Smart borrowers will lock in their interest rates. Sometimes interest rates will have gone up by the closing date, in which case, the lender will make less money than would have been made had you not locked in. Some lenders try to charge a yield spread fee to recoup some of this lost revenue, but this is not an industry-accepted business practice.

What is an Escrow Impound Account? How Can it Effect You?

Borrowers may be required by their lenders to put money into an escrow account as a prepayment of property taxes and insurances. The requirement may be up to the equivalent of two months' payments. If borrowers do not have this prepayment, they may not close.

What Insurances Will Be Required By the Lender?

As previously mentioned, borrowers can expect a lender to require at least fire insurance and homeowner's insurance. Flood insurance will be required in a flood plane. If the property is located in an area that routinely experiences natural disasters such as tornadoes or hurricanes, you may be asked to purchase supplemental homeowners' and flood insurance polices. You should consult with your lender in advance of making a purchase offer as the cost of these policies could diminish the monthly mortgage amount you can afford. Buyers would be wise to shop around because premiums can vary widely between companies. In 2006, in a developed area that did not routinely experience natural disasters the typical flood insurance premium was $700 a year. Because of the Katrina Disaster, most flood insurance policies required an up front payment in full. The typical homeowner's policy was $500 a year.

If more than 80 percent of the value of the property is borrowed, the lender will probably require mortgage insurance. Mortgage insurance protects the lender in the event of a foreclosure after the market has dropped, diminishing the property's value. You should note, mortgage insurance could allow buyers to put less money down, maintaining their savings. When securing mortgage insurance, borrowers normally pay an up front premium and then a percentage of the total loan each year. As the amount owed decreases so does the mortgage insurance payment.

How Do Homeowner's Insurances Work?

A home insurance policy is usually extended for a contracted term, a fixed period. Payments made to the insurer are called premiums or premium payments. The insured must pay the insurer the premium each term. Most insurers will give discounted premiums if it is less likely the property will be damaged or destroyed. For example, if the property is a fire station, or if the house is equipped with fire sprinklers and fire alarms, discounts may be given. Perpetual insurance, which is type of home insurance without a fixed term, can also be obtained in certain areas but is less common.

After a prospective property owner has applied for coverage with an insurance carrier, the carrier submits information to an underwriter. Insurance underwriters determine how risky it is to insure people and businesses and whether the carrier should accept the application at all. They also decide how much coverage should be received and how much should be paid for it. Underwriters can decide to exclude payment under certain circumstances on some policies. These stipulations are called exclusions. The underwriter can increase the premium charged to reflect the level of risk, called loading the premium. Like mortgage underwriting, insurance underwriting involves measuring risk exposure and determining the premium for insuring that risk.

The buyer will receive a certificate of insurance after the decision has been made to issue a policy. This certificate is promise of insurance in the event of a loss.

Insurance carriers protect themselves with reinsurance. Reinsurance works in exactly the same way as your insurance but on a larger scale. For example, if your house is destroyed in a certain year but almost every other house in your state is unaffected, the premiums paid by those other policyholders in your state will cover the cost of rebuilding your house and create a profit for the insurance carrier. However, carriers have problems when catastrophic events destroy large areas because the premium payments of others will not cover the total cost. Therefore, the company itself must buy insurance against that event. Reinsurers operate on a global scale out of the necessity to spread losses over multiple countries. Reinsurers would be affected only by a global catastrophe.

Homeowner's insurances really became popular during the 1950s. However, the policies were not standardized. Each carrier offered a dramatically different plan, making comparative shopping and risk assessment difficult. This was such a problem that in 1971 the New Jersey Insurance Services Office was formed to offer risk information and sell a standardized plan as a wholesaler to independent carriers. It originally sold six policies. Today, three are commonly used, HO-3, HO-6 and HO-4. HO-4 is renter's insurance. HO-3 is the most common for homeowners and is designed to cover all aspects of the home, structure, and its contents. Additionally, it covers the property owners from liability claims made by visitors. The coverage is usually called "all risk" or an "open perils" policy.

HO-6 is condominium coverage. It gives coverage only for the part of the building owned by the insured and is designed to span the gap between what the homeowner's association might cover in a blanket policy written for an entire neighborhood and the homeowner's personal property. Typically HO-6 also covers liability for guests of the insured. The policy can cover valuables within the condo from theft, fire, or water damage. Before getting this policy, you should find out what the homeowner's association already covers.

What are the Basic Types of Loans?

Most buyers will get a conventional loan. Conventional Loans are all loans not guaranteed by either Federal Housing Administration (FHA) or the Veterans Affairs (VA). When a loan is guaranteed, someone or some agency has agreed to repay the loan if the borrower defaults.

Conventional loans fall into two categories: The first are conforming loans for less than $417,000. The second are non-conforming loans for more than $417,000. Non-conforming loans are also known as jumbo loans.

Low to moderate income individuals and those with less than excellent credit who have failed to qualify for conventional financing can apply for an **FHA Loan**. These loans are made by regular financial institutions but are guaranteed by the Federal Housing Administration. However, the FHA has stringent qualification guidelines that must be met before they guarantee a loan. Unfortunately, many institutions find the process to be too time-consuming and choose not to participate. For this reason, buyers who plan to go the FHA route should obtain prequalification before making a purchase offer. In addition, FHA borrowers are not permitted to pay many of the fees that are traditionally picked up by borrowers. Potential borrowers should get clear instructions regarding fees from the FHA office.

VA Loans, guaranteed by the Veterans Affairs Department, are very similar to FHA loans but are made to active duty or retired military personnel. The VA does not have any funds to loan but guarantees financial institutions against loss. Buyers who plan to get VA loans should also plan to obtain prequalification because the loan process is lengthy. In addition, VA borrowers are not permitted to pay many of the fees that are traditionally picked up by borrowers, including inspection fees. Potential borrowers should get clear instructions regarding fees from the VA office.

Fannie Mae Loans, also known as the Community Home Buyer's Program, is sponsored by the federal government and offered only to first-time home buyers of middle and lower incomes. A credit check will not be requested; instead, borrowers must show good faith by presenting a record of utility bills and rent paid on time. Borrowers are usually allowed to have a small down payment of only three percent to five percent. The program also does not require a checking or savings account reserve. Conventional loans usually do.

Construction Loans are the fourth type of basic loan. They are short-term loans, of usually 12 to 18 months used to build a structure. They are typically made at prime rate. Prime rate is the lowest rate of interest charged by commercial banks. The prime rate is offered only to the most creditworthy customers and only on certain types of loans. Normally only the most creditworthy customers or those who already own a property outright will be approved for a construction loan. This is because the lender must lend with nothing to sell except the land if the borrower defaults. Usually construction loan payments are applied to the interest only. The loan is closed when the structure is completed.

How Do Adjustable and Variable Interest Rates Work?

Variable or Adjustable Rate Mortgages (ARMS) have fixed rates only for a short period and not for the entire life of the loan. After the initial fixed period, the rate will adjust to a new and usually higher rate periodically according to the terms set when the loan originated. The rate will be based on a specific index, which today is usually the LIBOR rate which stands for London Interbank Offered Rate, the interest rate offered by many London Banks for dollar deposits. These deposits are generally made for one-, three-, six-, or twelve-month periods. An ARM will adjust in accordance with one of these periods.

Borrowers should be aware that if the required interest rate increase exceeds the borrower's payment cap, negative amortization would result.

TIP

Buyers should be careful when using ARMs because although they have a cap on each periodic change, meaning the borrower has been guaranteed that the rate will not rise above a predetermined amount, when the rate changes the payment will change as well. Buyers must be aware that the change will usually be higher. They need to be prepared and ready for the change. Adjustable rate mortgages are usually only recommended when rates are high and might come down in the near future or when a buyer does not intend to occupy the property longer than the term of the fixed period (the buyer intends to "flip" the property for a profit shortly after its purchase).

What is the Truth in Lending Act and How Does It Protect Borrowers?

The Truth in Lending Act is a revision of an old law regarding financing the purchase of residences. The Act is also applicable to home equity loans or lines of credit in which the Act gives the borrower the right to back out before the loan is closed. It dictates that certain information must be given to the borrower before closing. In general, disclosure is required before any closed end credit transaction is completed. Closed end credit is the opposite of open-end credit, such as credit cards where payment in full is not expected at a predetermined date in the future. There is an exception when credit is extended by phone or mail. In those cases, a disclosure may be made after the fact. Some lenders will complete the disclosure and some will leave it up to the closing title agent or the closing attorney.

The Act is broken into two regulations, Z and M. Regulation Z applies to each individual or business that offers or extends consumer credit if four conditions are met: The credit is offered to consumers. The credit is offered on a regular basis. The credit is subject to a finance charge or must be paid in more than four installments according to a written agreement. The credit is primarily for personal, family, or household purposes.

If credit is extended for a business, commercial, or agricultural purpose, Regulation Z does not apply. Regulation M applies to contracts in the form of a bailment or lease where personal property will be used by a person primarily for personal, family, or household purposes. Regulation M does not apply to the subject matter of this book.

The following list of disclosures must be made to the borrower.

- Name of Lender

- Amount Financed

- An Itemization of the Amount Financed

- Finance Charges

- Annual Percentage Rate

- Variable Rate (When Applicable)

- Payment Schedule

- Total of Each Payment to be Made

- Explanation of How Payment will be Demanded

- Prepayment Penalities (When Applicable)

- Late Payment Penalities

- Security Interest

- Insurance

- Security Interest Change

- Contract Reference

- Assumption Policy (Assumption is discussed in Chapter 6)

- Required Deposits

The Act is designed to protect borrowers by requiring that certain information be disclosed before the promissory note is signed. A creditor who violates the disclosure requirements may be sued for twice the amount of the finance charge. Attorney's fees may also be awarded to the consumer. A lawsuit must be initiated by the consumer within a year of the violation.

Why Should a Buyer Have Representation?

A buyer may want to hire a real estate agent for the same reasons a seller might. First, the buyer has access to the advice of an experienced person. As the first case study on the following page demonstrates, mistakes in areas such as valuation can be costly to you as a buyer. Second, if you do not hire an agent, you will have to do all of the (quite extensive) work yourself. Please refer to section 1.01 for a description of the agent's role.

Compare the next two case studies. You will see the buying experience of someone with good representation.

Should the Buyer Designate "Power of Attorney?"

A "power of attorney" is a document that allows you to appoint a person or organization to handle your affairs while you are unavailable or unable to do so. The person or organization you appoint is referred to as an "attorney-in-fact" or "agent." Deciding to designate power of attorney is a personal choice. When making this decision, consider that a seller with an outstanding backup offer may be more motivated to hold you to the designated closing date. Certainly, buyers traveling a great distance to attend closing should consider this option fully.

Case Study: Eric Bozinny

This story exemplifies the importance of solid valuation. Purchase mistakes made because of valuation errors can create a significant loss for the buyer, leaving the buyer struggling to find a way out of the deal.

This acquisition will probably be my most costly mistake since we started investing. At this point I don't see a profitable exit out of this property. There were three options: sell as is, build and sell, or prepare and sell. All will mean losses. The decision I had to make was finding the exit

Case Study: Eric Bozinny

that would cost me the least money. Selling "as is" will not require additional capital, but doing so will not find a buyer without a significant reduction in price, resulting in a $50,000 loss. Building did not make sense, since land and construction costs will top out at more than the market price of the finished product. However, a middle ground I am pursuing is to pay to have the site developed, get it ready to build, and market it as such. This way, the option for me to build is still open.

Case Study: Eric Terry and Roger Blain

This is story of how easy a purchase can be with the assistance of expert representation.

Our purchase happened fast and easy. We prequalified about one month before we bought the property. We hired our own real estate agent. An agent can only look out for one interest at a time so that each party should have their own. We also hired an attorney who checked the title for liens. The attorney checked the property for overdue back taxes and represented our interests. A title agent did perform the title search, but the attorney arranged it. The attorney also handled the closing. He obtained copies of utility bills and prorated them for us. We showed up at his office and all of our documents were ready for us.

PROPERTY BUYER'S CHECKLIST

- Property address.

- Asking price.

- Square footage.

- Residential zoning?

- Is the property close to work, school, shopping, medical facilities, places of worship, parks, and public transportation?

- What is the overall exterior and interior condition upon general visual Inspection?

PROPERTY BUYER'S CHECKLIST

- Will you have adequate storage space?
- How is the building constructed (wood, block, brick)?
- Can you extend the building?
- Type of heating and cooling—estimated monthly bill.
- What are the real estate taxes?
- Number of bathrooms and bedrooms.
- What are the ages of the heating and cooling systems,
- Are appliances included? Offered "as is"? Include condition of each.
- What is the capacity of the water heater?
- Have utilities been installed?
- Does the building have enough electrical outlets/ phone jacks?
- What is the age of the electrical wiring?
- What is the condition of the plumbing?
- Does the property have street lights, alleys, sidewalks? Include condition?
- What is the volume of traffic near the building?
- Is the property near industry? Will you be exposed to noise or pollution?
- Are the neighboring properties well maintained?

BUYER'S FLOWCHART

#1	Choose a real estate broker	Choose a real estate attorney or a title agent	Choose a mortgage broker
#2	↓	↓	Mortgage prequalification
#3	Choose a property	↓	↓
#4	Create a Purchase Offer (RE Agent or Attny.), Go into Escrow	Create a Purchase Offer (RE Agent or Attny.), Go into Escrow	↓

#5	Assists with planning of inspections & walkthroughs	Conducts title search, works to settle title problems	Arranges appraisal
#6	↓	↓	Finalizes mortgage, obtains insurance certificates
#7	Receives a commission fee	Arranges closing documents, oversees closing, arranges the payment of fees	Might receive a commission fee

MONTHLY EXPENSES WORKSHEET

	PROPERTY		PERSONAL EXPENSES
$_____.___	Mortgage Payment	$_____.___	Food
$_____.___	Taxes & Insurance	$_____.___	Clothing
$_____.___	Routine Maintenance	$_____.___	Gifts/Donations
$_____.___	**Sub-Total**	$_____.___	Personal Allowances
		$_____.___	Pet Expenses
	UTILITIES	$_____.___	Medical
$_____.___	Heating & Cooling	$_____.___	Prescriptions
$_____.___	Water	$_____.___	Vacation
$_____.___	Electricity	$_____.___	Educational Expenses
$_____.___	Gas	$_____.___	Investment Contributions
$_____.___	Phone	$_____.___	**Sub-Total**
$_____.___	Cable		
$_____.___	Internet		**OTHER**
$_____.___	Garbage Removal	$_____.___	Debts
	Laundry/	$_____.___	Fixed Financial
$_____.___	Cleaning Service	$_____.___	Obligations
$_____.___	Automobile Expenses	$_____.___	Other
$_____.___	**Sub-Total**	$_____.___	**Sub-Total**
	$_____.___ **Grand Total**		

chapter two

The Offer

Section 2.01: Understanding the Purchase Offer

Negotiating the Purchase

The purchase offer is a formal and legally binding document. Buyers and sellers frequently do preliminary negotiating in advance of drawing up the purchase offer. Each negotiation is different, as it involves different people, each with their own ideas of how it should proceed. Sometimes parties will have direct contact. In other cases, all discussions will take place between the real estate agents.

Salespeople have written books explaining how one person can "trick" another person during the negotiation process. I negotiated my own deal during my most recent purchase and bought the property below market value. I am not a sales person. I do not know any tricks. I simply met with the seller. I listened to him. I found out what he wanted to get from this deal. As things turned out, he had bought the property as an investment and had certain financial goals in mind. He had attempted to rent the property with limited success and now owed back taxes. His tenants had done some interesting decorating that he did not want to fix. My husband and I had financial goals also and needed to buy a house that would not take us off track. In the end, we agreed to do the repairs and pay the overdue taxes. He compromised on the price, but still made a nice profit on the house. My husband and I got our house in the neighborhood we wanted without breaking the bank. The approach I used is sometimes called the win-win approach. During the 20th century, psychologists developed ideas suggesting that agreements frequently can be reached if parties look at their underlying interests and needs instead of their stated positions.

After a deal is agreed upon, buyers should have the purchase contract signed as quickly as possible. Having the main parts of the contract drawn up in advance is an advantage. The housing market can be a competitive place. Securing your deal just makes sense.

> **TIP**
>
> Chapter 1, Section 1.04 contains a "buyer's checklist" of ideas to consider when touring a property. If any of these items are less than what you had hoped but not enough to make you pass on the property, use them as negotiating tools. Take notes during the tour and review your list when you are preparing to negotiate.

Unfortunately, you may run into some unscrupulous people in your real estate dealings. Always keep your eyes open. I once had my heart set on a gorgeous red brick 1950s house. I phoned my agent who agreed to meet for a tour. When we arrived at the property, things quickly turned sour. My agent recognized an agent who was already there giving a tour. She knew he had a reputation so she did some checking. As things turned out, he was a 50 percent owner. However, he had not told the potential buyers, whom he was representing, that he was essentially representing both sides. Later, we discovered he had given numerous tours while positioning himself as an agent to the buyers, to whip up a bidding war and drive up the final selling price of his property. In this situation an experienced agent who knows the ins and outs of the local market can protect you.

Negotiating the Sale

People who are "just looking" are aggravating obstacles to sellers. Nothing is worse than investing an entire Sunday in a house full of lookers. A good real estate agent will screen and separate potential buyers from lookers at the door, helping the lookers to realize they should move along. Self-sellers will need to handle this themselves. Initiating a conversation about the buyer's mortgage prequalification is a good technique. It serves two purposes: lookers will be encouraged to leave and sellers can find prequalified buyers. Dealing with a prequalified buyer is in the seller's best interest because the deal will be less likely to fall through.

If buyer negotiations are not going well, introduce an intermediary, sometimes called the advocate approach, based on the work of Mary Parker Follett who advanced the idea of "reciprocal relationships" in understanding the dynamic aspects of the individual in relationship to others. Understandably, buyers will be hesitant to tell you what they hate about your house or to see any position other than their own. If buyers are stymied by cosmetic issues, unable to see that these things are changeable, or if they express their dislike to you, negotiations may stop suddenly. Sometimes the buyer simply needs to move on. Sometimes a small price reduction will make all the difference. A third party may be able to flush out the problem.

A seller should also consider bringing in an intermediary when a final price cannot be agreed on, especially true when offers are consistently lower than the asking price. Sellers can become emotionally attached to their properties, viewing them through rose-colored glasses and overpricing them.

An appraisal is a great leg for a seller to stand on during the negotiation process; and it will make your offer more attractive for two reasons. First, nobody wants to buy a property that cannot resell to break even. Second, no one wants to make a purchase offer only to discover the property will not appraise well.

Earnest Money

Upon submitting the formal purchase offer, buyers are expected to give earnest money to indicate the offer is sincere. Be certain to include in the purchase offer the provision that this money will be applied to the sale price. The industry does not have hard and fast rules regarding how much should be exchanged. Sometimes new buyers have difficulty deciding how much to offer. An experienced real estate agent can give some guidance. In general terms, the earnest money should be in line with the cost of the property. Keep in mind that under some circumstances this money can be forfeited. Do not give so much that you are unable to make another purchase offer later should this deal fall through and you lose the earnest money.

Some sellers, specifically those selling higher priced homes, respond to the purchase offer with a request for additional earnest money before closing but after the completion of the inspections. This is not abnormal or considered to be out of line within the industry. Houses tend to sell for less after they have been on the market for over one month. Real estate agents sometimes call this spoilage. This occurs because buyers assume the seller has become desperate to sell and offer less. Understandably, individuals selling luxury properties have more to lose should the buyer back out. They are looking for reassurance that you still plan to go forward with the deal after the property has been inspected. If you have any suspicion that you may need to back out, do not give the second sum, obviously.

Checks for earnest money should be made out to the escrow company. A more detailed explanation of who handles the earnest money can be found in the following section.

Creating a Purchase Offer

The purchase offer is also known as the "contract of sale." It is used to suggest how the purchase will proceed. That sentence is very important. "How the purchase will proceed" means what rights will be granted to each party. In many ways, it is the most important step in the transaction process. The purchase offer must have mentally competent parties. It must have a valid consideration. This is the legal term for earnest money or money given by the buyer to indicate that the offer is made in good faith. The buyer cannot rescind the earnest money unless there is good cause. For example, the buyer would have good cause if the property were surveyed and found to be significantly smaller than advertised. In essence, the buyer would need to demonstrate that the property had been misrepresented in some way or that it had less value due to undisclosed information. The buyer would need to prove that the property was not what they had agreed to buy. Once earnest money has been given, another document called a "receipt for deposit" is created. Last, there must be a mutual agreement of the terms of the contract. This mutual agreement establishes the principals of the purchase. Examples of principals are the real estate agent, the buyer, the seller, representing attorneys, and the lender. Every purchase contract should have the following components.

Attorney Review Clause or Attorney Contingency Clause

The attorney review clause obligates the seller to give the buyer three business days to review the purchase contract with his or her attorney. If the attorney disapproves of any part of the contract, the contract can be broken until the other party agrees to change it or a compromise is negotiated.

Timing/Method of Payment

This is sometimes worded as "financial arrangements." This section should state the full purchase price. If the earnest money is counted as payment toward the purchase price, it should be stated in this clause. If the earnest money is to be made in installments, the terms should be laid out in this clause. The buyer must be given ample time to seek and be approved for financing. Typically, the buyer will be given a minimum of 30 days. This clause protects the buyer by defining the earnest money terms and allowing time to secure financing.

Date for the Close of Escrow

The expected date of closing and what will happen if this date is missed should be set forth. Otherwise, either party could be left hanging indefinitely or until a court is asked to intercede.

Stipulation for Payment of Real Estate Commissions

The terms of the division of real estate commissions are laid out here protecting both the buyer and seller from unpleasant surprises later.

Covenants, Conditions, and Restrictions (CC&Rs)

Any limitations placed on the property by the current owner, the local government, the homeowner's or condominium association, or any other governing body with right to lay restrictions on a title should be disclosed here. In some cases, a seller will not be aware of title CC&Rs. These unknown CC&Rs should be discovered during the title search. In fact, this is one of the purposes of the title search. However, the seller is legally obligated to disclose any known information.

Mortgage Contingency Clause

This clause releases the buyer from the sale in the event financing cannot be obtained. Without this clause, the buyer would be obligated to purchase the property even if financing could not be found.

Inspections Clause

This clause gives the buyer the right to have inspections by licensed professionals and to cancel the contract if those inspections are negative. It protects the seller by limiting the time for inspections and by placing criteria on the degree of defect that must be discovered before the contract can be voided. The buyer can be given active or passive approval within this clause. Passive approval means the buyer must disapprove of the inspection within a specified period or the seller will assume the inspection was approved. Active approval is, of course, the opposite. This clause should also state who would pay for needed repairs discovered during the inspection process. The buyer should protect himself or herself by putting a cap on the repair bills they will assume with the purchase.

Pre-Closing Damage/Destruction Clause

This clause protects the buyer by voiding the contract if the property is damaged or destroyed while in escrow. However, this clause is limited in some states. Buyers should consult with an attorney for details regarding their rights.

Prorations Clause

This clause protects both the buyer and seller by defining the terms under which monthly property bills incurred while the property is in escrow will be divided. These bills can include but are not limited to taxes and utilities.

Fixtures, Personal Property, and Bill of Sale Clause

This clause protects both the buyer and seller by defining which items the seller will leave on the property upon closing. This clause can cover items inside and outside a building. All items of significant value should be mentioned in this clause. Do not conjecture that the buyer will assume certain items are not included in the sale. Instead, assume the buyer thinks anything present during the initial tour will be included in the sale. Examples of items that commonly cause misunderstandings are appliances, light fixtures, above ground swimming pools, landscaping, and furniture built into the walls of the building such as bookshelves.

Post-Closing Possession Agreement

This section spells out the date the buyer will take possession of the property and how the transfer will be conducted. It can cause serious problems if it is overlooked. On a personal note, I was left homeless for four days after purchasing a new house because both the seller and the seller's agent thought I would be getting keys from the other. Both left for out of town vacations immediately after our closing. Other problems can occur if, for example, the seller cannot move out on or before closing day. Both parties should work out exactly when the seller will be moving out in advance for obvious reasons. The buyer and seller should work out a rental agreement in the event the seller opts to stay for an extended period.

Disclosure Contingency

Most states have seller disclosure laws. If your state does not, you must add a disclosure clause to the purchase agreement. This clause requires the seller to disclose any known defects or face fraud charges. An attorney or a licensed real estate agent can insert this clause for you.

Approval of Repair Work

The purchase contract should describe who would schedule and approve repair work deemed necessary during the inspection process. Buyers should designate themselves as the repair approval agent for obvious reasons.

Good and Marketable Title

Be certain your contract makes the sale contingent on a marketable title. Refer to Chapter 4, Section 4.02.

Liquidated Contingency Clause

This is a clause in the purchase contract that limits the judgment of a breach of contract lawsuit to actual damages. The party suing cannot request punitive damages.

Condominium/Association Letters and Waivers

Buyers should request a condominium or Homeowners Association warranty letter where applicable. A sample condo warranty letter is in the Appendix. Buyers want certain information about the property such as planned rate increases, planned renovations to public spaces, and planned construction. A warranty letter should request monthly association rates and the terms of insurance policies carried on public spaces. Please refer to the sample letter for additional information about its contents.

Right of First Refusal

In addition to a warranty letter, buyers should request a "waiver of the right to first refusal." In the absence of this waiver, an association could decline a buyer who is already in escrow.

Nonrecurring Closing Costs

Buyers may ask the seller to pay their nonrecurring closing costs. One way to ask is simply insert a clause into the purchase contract. Alternatively, the buyer can just ask. If the seller refuses to pay these fees and the buyer does not have the cash to cover them, they can be added to the final sale price and paid by the seller at closing, meaning the buyer really paid the fees just not up front. There are other ways to cover the closing such as taking out a second mortgage, but rolling the fees into the sale price is the least complicated and the least likely to cause your lender to raise an eyebrow. Keep in mind, the property must appraise high enough to cover this amount. Another option for cash-strapped buyers is to negotiate with the lender for a higher interest rate in exchange for "no-cost-financing" (discussed in detail in Chapter 6, Section 6.06). Obviously, it will cost substantially more in the end unless the loan is paid off early or the property is resold before the end of the mortgage. Nonrecurring closing costs include the title insurance charge, the escrow charge, points to be bought down at closing (see the "points" section for an explanation), attorney's fees, the appraisal fee, inspection fees, and any other one-time fees scheduled to be paid at closing.

After the seller receives the purchase contract, *written escrow* along with *closing instructions* are created and added to it. Being in escrow means money, property, a deed, or a bond are put into the custody of a third party for delivery to a grantee after fulfilling specified conditions. The specified conditions are the closing instructions. The written escrow also comes from this third party, which is a title or escrow company. An attorney or real estate agent may initiate opening escrow on the buyer's behalf. However, the buyer can hire their own title or escrow company if no other principals are involved. The escrow agent, sometimes referred to as an escrow officer, closer, closing agent or title officer, acts as an unbiased separate party when processing all of the closing documents. This person must answer the questions of all principals but is obligated to maintain reasonable confidentiality.

In some instances, the buyer and seller will not be able to agree upon the closing terms. In this situation they can choose to draw up an "escrow agreement," which gives instructions for parts of the escrow to be done after closing.

TIP Oral agreements among buyers, sellers, brokers, and agents are legally binding in a court of law.

Section 2.02: Other Issues to Consider

Estoppel Letters

There are two kinds of estoppel letters, also called estoppel certificates, An estoppel for a note will be discussed in Chapter 6. Here we deal with estoppels pertaining to leases.

When purchasing a rental property, buyers should always get an estoppel letter from the seller to protect buyers from unscrupulous tenants who may claim ownership of appliances or request non-existent security deposits. They spell out what the buyer is getting in black and white. The letter, drawn up by the seller or the seller's attorney and signed by the seller and the tenants, ***should contain all of the fundamental lease provisions*** such as the tenant's name, unit number, rent amount, rent due date, security deposit, late fees, type of tenancy, and any real property belonging to the facility. The letter must be signed by only the parties noted on the lease; otherwise, it may be voided. Buyers should read the letter carefully, verifying that all blanks have been filled in or marked N/A. I cannot stress this enough. In addition to the estoppel, a buyer should be provided with a copy of the original lease. The closing officer should prepare an "assignment of lease" form to be signed at the closing. This form transfers the lease to the new owner. Reassignment of leases is discussed in Chapter 5, The Closing. A sample of the assignment of lease form is available in the Appendix.

Case Study: Refer to Miner v. Tustin Avenue Investors

The buyer won the following case on appeal but had to fight a lengthy court battle to do so, which could have been prevented by carefully reading the lease and estoppel letter/certificate prior to closing.

In this case, the tenant had an extension

Case Study: Refer to Miner v. Tustin Avenue Investors

option on the lease. This option was noted on the lease but not on the estoppel certificate, which the tenant signed. To be more exact, the estoppel contained the statement "except: _____", which the tenant failed to fill in. The buyer refused to honor the lease extension and litigation ensued. A court of appeals treated the estoppel certificate as a continuation of the lease and denied the tenant the extension option.

What is the Importance of the Walkthrough?

The seller may be living in another state, or the property may be occupied by a tenant. Whatever the reason given, sellers will sometimes try to convince buyers to forgo a walkthrough. I have personally had associates who purchased properties sight unseen. Traditionally, the buyer will get a minimum of one initial walkthrough and another immediately before closing. Insist on your right to two walkthroughs. I think the following case study speaks for itself.

Case Study: Eric Bozinny

This account demonstrates why a buyer should get an estoppel letter, review the tenant lease, and insist on conducting a walkthrough inspection.

Our first property was one that turned out to be a real headache. Let me list all the issues with this property.

- Squatters

- Seven cars abandoned in backyard

- A complete dump of a house

The tenant never ended up paying any rent, abandoned the property, but all his drug using friends stayed behind. After two months and a couple of court appearances, we finally got them out.

chapter three

You are in Escrow. Now What?

Section 3.01: Seller's Disclosures

The disclosure is a tricky area for the seller. Not every state requires the seller to make a full written disclosure. However, many real estate associations recommend it to their members, and many attorneys think it supplies the buyer with one more piece of evidence should litigation ensue. What really is in the seller's best interest?

Look at this from the buyer's perspective. If negative information is disclosed, the buyer may back out of the deal. Certainly, the buyer will conduct inspections during which the buyer will probably find out the problem anyway. If the seller is not up front from the beginning, how much more likely will the buyer be to break the deal?

If the seller does not disclose and the inspector does not discover the issue, the buyer may discover it after closing, especially if the buyer plans to live at the property. After closing, the seller is open to litigation. Should the seller gamble that the buyer would bring a lawsuit? How much could the seller lose in a lawsuit? After taking legal fees and lost work time into consideration, how can one assume the result would cost less than the original repair or disclosure? Obviously, disclosure is in the best interest of both parties. If the seller does not offer a disclosure, the seller should ask for one.

Section 3.02: Inspections

Most lenders will require at least a building inspection and a pest and termite inspection. Traditionally, the buyer will schedule and pay for them. *However, VA Home Mortgage Loans do not allow borrowers to pay any inspection fees (Refer to Chapter 1, Section 1.04).* Buyers can request other inspections such as a separate roof, electrical, and plumbing inspection, but a pest, termite, and building inspection are standard. The pest and termite inspections should be done promptly to allow time to resolve problems before closing. Because these inspections will need to be completed before your scheduled closing date, schedule them right away; do not procrastinate. Pest inspection fees vary but expect to pay at least $50. The building inspection, which is based on the size of the building, will vary from $150 to $500 but is well worth the money considering the potential cost of serious undiscovered repairs. Buyers should plan to accompany the inspectors to ask questions and to form a solid understanding of what was discovered, which would be important should negotiations ensue. Any of the principals of the escrow can schedule the inspections. However, the buyer would be serving his or her best interests by scheduling an independent inspector or allowing the representing real estate agent to do it.

Inspectors can be located easily through an Internet or yellow pages search. You should ask for references, find out how long the company has been in business, and get the fee rates. If you are still in doubt, check with the better business bureau for a listing of complaints made against the company. Buyers can also check with ASHI (American Society of Home Inspectors). ASHI is a national non-profit professional association. Their web address is **www.ashi.com**. Members must have performed at least 750 inspections or 250 inspections in conjunction with a written test. Additionally, they must submit three referrals from other members and satisfactorily complete an inspection under the supervision of a board member. The National Association of Home Inspectors (NAHI) is another professional association that could serve as a resource, but their admittance criteria are not as stringent as ASHI. Their web address is **www.nahi.com**.

Avoid price shopping when searching for an inspector. A home is the most expensive commodity you are likely to purchase and or sell in a lifetime. One defect missed by your inspector could cost 100 times what you saved with a bargain inspection.

Termite and Pest Inspections

The termite inspection should cover the following: wood damage, fungus, dry rot, faulty grade levels, earth-wood contacts, water leaks, cellulose debris on the subsoil — a possible termite sign — excessive moisture in the roof crawl space, evidence of subterranean termites, dry wood termites, damp wood termites, and other pests. The inspector's report should include suggested corrective work or needed preventative work and a price quote. Inspectors must be board certified and any previous reports filed with the board should be made available to the buyer as part of the inspection. The inspector should provide a guarantee also and give the buyer a written report.

Buyers should be wary of termite inspectors specifically. Remember this person has not only inspected the property but stands to make a sum of money if the seller agrees to do his or her suggested repairs. Therefore, this individual's best interests are served by finding necessary repairs and recommending the most expensive solution. This would not be done necessarily to hurt the buyer, but it may if your closing is held up or falls through completely. This is why choosing reputable inspector is so important. In this situation the seller, as suggested in the "seller's perspective" section, can help both parties by having their own termite and pest inspection report. Of course, the seller will have to pay for this extra inspection, but it is a good alternative to being taken for a ride.

Building Inspections

Because the purchase of a property probably represents the largest investment you will make during your lifetime, you should have inspections performed. As mentioned previously, buyers should schedule an inspection immediately after the purchase contract has been accepted. Typically, an inspection will take from two to eight hours depending on the size of the building and its components and will require another two to eight hours of document preparation. These documents should be given to both the buyer and seller by the inspector. Buyers should plan to be present for the inspection to ask questions and receive detailed information about any recommended repairs.

On inspection day the inspector explains the procedure and asks if the client has any special questions or requests. The client will be presented with an inspection agreement that outlines what will be reviewed. After it has been agreed to, the inspector will begin a walkthrough with the client. This will involve inspecting all visible and accessible areas, including the heating system, central air conditioning system, interior plumbing and electrical systems, roof, attic space, all visible insulation, the walls, ceilings, floors, doors, windows, basement or crawl space, and the foundation as well as all building attachments and out buildings. A check of the entire outlying property must be made to verify its condition and check for issues like expansive soils that are known to expand and contract causing structural problems through differential movement of the structure. Sample inspection forms can be found in the Appendix.

Last, the inspector will complete the inspection report. All deficiencies and maintenance recommendations will be noted and a description of those deficiencies will be entered onto the summary sheet of the report for the client.

A common question asked of inspectors is, "How long will such and such last?" A home inspector does not have any accurate method to determine exactly how long a particular system or component will last. In most instances, there are simply too many variables to determine the life span of items that require routine maintenance and have thousands of integral components. The following items should be covered in a home inspection. This list is a general overview. It is not comprehensive and cannot serve as an inspection substitute.

Grounds

Ideally, water drainage should move away from buildings. The property should have a water containment setup if large amounts of drainage are anticipated. Check for erosion, a symptom of improper drainage, around building foundations. While performing this inspection, check for signs of previous leakage into basements and crawl spaces as well as resulting deterioration. Inspect the condition of walkways, driveways, steps, railings, fences, and landscaping. Retaining walls should be inspected for structural fatigue and signs of ongoing water erosion.

Structural

Inspect foundations, walls, basements, roofs, chimneys, decks, porches, and patios for signs of structural fatigue or water and weather erosion. Note the structural integrity of garages and other out buildings.

Exterior

Note the condition of outdoor areas that are exposed to the weather such as doors, windows, siding, gutters, soffits, hoses, and outdoor electrical outlets. Check that outdoor outlets have been grounded. Inspect the condition of outdoor paint and caulking. Note structural damage resulting from ill-kept paint and caulking. Evaluate the condition of built-in outdoor furniture, landscaping fixtures such as terracing, pools and other water fixtures, and large non-portable pieces of playground equipment that will remain after the sale.

Interior

Note the working condition of stairs, railings, windows, doors, ceiling fans, appliances, lights, and fireplaces. Inspect walls, interior paint, caulking for age deterioration. Inspect the working condition of heaters and cooling systems as well as their corresponding thermostats. Check that the walls, floors, and crawl spaces have adequate insulation. Check that the windows have energy conserving glass.

Plumbing

Note the condition of pipes, drains, fixtures, and the water heater. Check the water heater's emergency ventilation system for safety. Check for adequate water pressure. Note the piping material and if it is safe and sufficient to handle ongoing water pressure. Test water fixtures for leaks and improper installation. Check that pipes extending to the outside have sufficient insulation.

Electrical

Check that all electrical wiring follows commercial safety standards and that all outlets have been grounded and have appropriate sheathing. Note the amperage service to all buildings and if it is sufficient to meet the buyer's purposes.

Maintenance

Comment on the overall maintenance condition of the property and buildings.

Environmental Testing

The following environmental tests should be conducted:

- Evaluation of the Incoming Water Quality
- Radon
- Lead Paint Testing
- Mold Testing
- Asbestos
- Septic Evaluation

Earthquakes

Buildings should be evaluated for their ability to withstand earthquakes in areas where this is applicable. If found to be deficient, the buyer can request, "retrofitting" to bring the building up to modern standards. However, this is very expensive. Do not be surprised if it breaks the deal.

Case Study: Noelle Matzek

The following wonderfully informative story was donated by a first time home buyer who is an associate of mine.

During the inspection process, be certain to test large appliances and look under and behind them. It became apparent within our first few days of occupancy that we needed to replace the fridge. The door hinge was bent allowing cold air to leak out. We bought a new fridge and had it delivered. As we moved the old one out of the way, we discovered it did not have a drip pan beneath it to catch the excess water released by the auto defrost cycle. The two walls the refrigerator was up against had deteriorated where they meet the floor and needed to be patched with new drywall.

Our home was the model home for a 1950s development project. Our house was built in 1951. The roof consists of planks covered with ½" plywood, and tar paper which was covered with a white roof coating. In the majority of

Case Study: Noelle Matzek

the house, the ceiling is drywall that is attached directly to the roof planks, meaning no air space or insulation between the ceiling and the roof itself. The effect is a very hot house in the summer and a cold house in the winter. Furthermore, the house was not built with window eves or rain gutters.

Our house was originally two buildings, a sales office and a model home. At some point the sales office and the model home were connected. I believe the sales office was never meant to be part of a permanent residence, and whatever method was used to connect the two buildings was not up to par. We have experienced leakage problems at the connection points. We would love to expand part of the house, but because the two patch worked buildings were connected without building permits and possibly violate codes, I have been told getting permits would be almost impossible unless we knocked down a section of the house and rebuilt from scratch.

The inspection process did reveal numerous issues as I have just listed here, but because I was a first time buyer relying on my real estate agent's experience to help us make sound decisions, I ignored them. She advised us to pick just a few issues and make requests of the seller to fix or replace those few things, letting the rest go. I regret that I took her advice and did not negotiate with the seller for more repairs. It never hurts to ask to have all the issues acknowledged. A few other issues I should have brought up were major plumbing problems in the bathroom that ultimately meant a complete renovation and a ground level clean out of the incoming and outgoing pipes. This repair involved digging up the back yard and removing a section of our porch. Needless to say, it was costly. Upon purchase, our house still had the original fuse box, which was grossly outdated. In addition, the grounds lacked shade of any kind.

When we bought the house, the kitchen had been only partially remodeled. It had no garbage disposal or dishwasher. While in and of itself this was not a concern at the walkthrough, unbeknownst to us there is no space for a normal size dishwasher, something the former owner must have realized during the renovation process. We have purchased and will be installing a 19" dishwasher, which will be inadequate for our family of four.

One piece of advice I can give is to look for signs of occupancy. Ask if the house is being "flipped." If the current owners are not living in the house, they could easily be motivated to make superficial upgrades that will not

Case Study: Noelle Matzek

withstand everyday use. We were told our house was occupied, but I doubt it. Some indications we saw that people were not living here were everyday bathroom items stored in the kitchen; no real food in the supposed home of a family of four; no bookcases or other storage space, and no shelving in the base cabinets in the kitchen.

Do a walkthrough inspection immediately before closing and do not hesitate to request immediate possession after closing. Upon moving in, we discovered the carpet in what would become my son's bedroom was saturated in cat urine.

Inspection Forms

The following are examples of home inspection forms. They were provided by and reprinted with the permission of Fred Ugast of Home Tech.

STRUCTURAL

TYPE PF BUILDING	□ Single □ Duplex □ Row house/Townhouse □ Multi-Unit □ Gable Roof □ Shed □ Hip □ Gambrel □ Mansard □ Flat □ Other _____
STRUCTURE	Foundation: □ Poured Concrete □ Block □ Brick □ Brick & Block □ Other _____ Posts/Columns: □ Steel □ Masonry □ Wood □ Concrete □ Not Visible Floor Structure _____ Wall Structure _____ Roof Structure _____ Water Damage: □ Some Signs □ Extensive □ None Observed □ No major structural defects noted-in normal condition for age

BASEMENT (OR LOWER LEVEL)

BASEMENT	□ Full □ Partial □ None □ Slab Grade Walls: □ Open □ Closed Ceiling: □ Open □ Closed □ Limited visibility due to extensive basement storage

FLOOR	☐ Concrete ☐ Dirt ☐ _____ ☐ Resilient Tile ☐ Sheet goods ☐ Carpeting ☐ _____ ☐ Satisfactory ☐ N/A
FLOOR DRAIN	☐ Tested ☐ Not Tested ☐ Water Observed in Crock Pipes: ☐ Copper ☐ Galvanized ☐ Plastic ☐ _____ ☐ Satisfactory ☐ N/A
BASEMENT DAMPNESS	☐ Some Signs ☐ Extensive ☐ Past ☐ Present ☐ Not Known ☐ None Observed
CRAWL SPACE	☐ Readily Accessible ☐ Not Readily Accessible ☐ Not Inspected ☐ Conditions Inspected ☐ Method: _____ Floor: ☐ Concrete ☐ Dirt ☐ _____ Dampness: ☐ Some Signs ☐ Extensive ☐ None Observed ☐ Vapor Barrier ☐ Insulation ☐ Ventilation
Remarks	

ROOFING SYSTEM

ROOF COVERING	Location Materials Age _____ _____ _____ _____ _____ _____ _____ _____ _____ How Inspected: _____ Roof Leaks: ☐ Some Signs ☐ Extensive ☐ None Observed
FLASHING	☐ Aluminum ☐ Galvanized ☐ Copper ☐ Rubberized Membrane ☐ _____ ☐ Satisfactory ☐ N/A
GUTTERS AND DOWNSPOUTS	☐ Aluminum ☐ Galvanized ☐ Copper ☐ Vinyl ☐ Wood Extensions: ☐ Yes ☐ No ☐ Satisfactory ☐ N/A

EXTERIOR

EXTERIOR DOORS	☐ Satisfactory
WINDOWS AND SKYLIGHTS	☐ Satisfactory

EXTERIOR WALL COVERING	_____ _____ ☐ Satisfactory _____ _____ ☐ Satisfactory _____ _____ ☐ Satisfactory _____ _____ ☐ Satisfactory
EXTERIOR TRIM	☐ Eaves ☐ Fascia ☐ Soffits ☐ Rake ☐ Signs of deterioration ☐ Extensive ☐ None observed ☐ Satisfactory
CHIMNEY	☐ Brick ☐ Metal ☐ Block ☐ _____ ☐ In Chase ☐ Flue liner partially observed ☐ Clean before use ☐ Satisfactory ☐ N/A
GARAGE/ CARPORT	☐ Garage ☐ Carport ☐ Attached ☐ Detached ☐ Door Opener ☐ Operating ☐ Safety Reverse ☐ Satisfactory ☐ N/A
PORCH	Floor: ☐ Wood ☐ Concrete ☐ _____ ☐ Railing/Guardrail ☐ Satisfactory ☐ N/A
Remarks:	

HEATING

HEATING SYSTEM	Fuel: ☐ Gas ☐ Oil ☐ Electric ☐ _____ ☐ Forced Air Furnace ☐ Gravity hot water boiler ☐ Forced hot water boiler ☐ Steam Boiler ☐ _____ ☐ Radiant Heat ☐ Electric Baseboard ☐ Heat Pump No. 1 Capacity: _____ Age: _____Yrs. No. 2 Capacity: _____ Age: _____Yrs. No. 3 Capacity: _____ Age: _____Yrs. When turned on by thermostat: ☐ Fired ☐ Did not fire
FUEL SUPPLY	☐ Oil Tank in Basement ☐ Buried ☐ _____ ☐ Public Gas Supply ☐ Tank ☐ Electricity ☐ _____ Fuel Supply Shutoff Location _____
HEAT EXCHANGER	☐ Partially observed ☐ Not visible, enclosed combustion ☐ Have Condition Checked Before Settlement ☐ N/A

HEAT DISTRIBUTION	☐ Radiators ☐ Convectors ☐ Baseboard convectors ☐ Radiant Pipes: ☐ Galvanized ☐ Copper ☐ Black Iron ☐ Pipes not visible ☐ Ductwork Heat source in each room ☐ Yes ☐ No
HUMIDIFIER	☐ Atomizer ☐ Evaporator ☐ Steam ☐ Not functioning ☐ Not tested ☐ N/A
FILTER	☐ Washable ☐ Disposable ☐ Electronic ☐ N/A
SUPPLEMENTARY HEAT	Location Type _____ _____ ☐ Satisfactory _____ _____ ☐ Satisfactory _____ _____ ☐ Satisfactory

COOLING

COOLING	☐ Cooling system integral with heating system ☐ Central Air ☐ Room Units ☐ Heat Pump ☐ Through-Wall ☐ Electric Compressor ☐ Gas Chiller ☐ Air Filter ☐ Air Handler ☐ Thermostat ☐ Satisfactory ☐ N/A No. 1 Condensing Unit Capacity: _____ Age: ____ Yrs. No. 2 Condensing Unit Capacity: _____ Age: ____ Yrs. No. 1 Condensing Unit Capacity: _____ Age: ____ Yrs. ☐ Tested ☐ Not Tested ☐ Ductwork ☐ Window units not tested
Remarks:	

What Happens When Lead Paint is Discovered During the Inspection ?

Lead based household paints were widely sold prior to 1978. Consequently, if you purchase a property constructed before 1978 in which the walls have not been completely sanded, chances are the building contains lead paint. If your inspector reports the presence of lead paint, you certainly are not alone. If the seller knows of the existence of lead paint, it must be reported to you in accordance with federal law. Choosing to go ahead with the purchase is purely a personal decision. Undoubtedly, the presence of children will make the decision more difficult. On one hand, it does not present a threat so long as it remains under at least one coat of non-lead based paint. On the other hand, paint does not last forever and you may find yourself dealing with the removal at some point in the future. Know this, at closing you will be expected to sign a waiver, forfeiting your right to any future restitution.

Building Codes

A typical buyer's inspection is focused on gathering information about the property for the client. The general home inspector is aware of the local codes, and the inspection report will consider them, especially if they have obviously been neglected. However, the scope of a general home inspection is targeted at providing an informative, detailed, and objective evaluation of the property.

If the buyer has reason to question whether building codes were followed, he or she should contact a code inspector. A failure to follow building codes during the construction process can result in the future inability to add additions or make renovations. Code inspectors work for their local municipality and enforce the local and state codes with little or no concern for the buyer's understanding of these codes. A code inspection does not communicate whether the house was well constructed. Therefore, a code inspection is very different from a home inspection and one cannot replace the other.

Should a New Construction Buyer Hire an Inspector?

Home buyers entering into a contract for the building of their new house should retain the services of a professional home inspector during the construction because they need to know that someone is looking out for them with independent, unbiased professional eyes. Once built, many conditions that could have been observed during the construction are now covered and no longer visible for inspection causing a potential financial burden for the property owner when future corrective action is required. Regardless of how well it is constructed or how reputable the construction company, the construction of a house involves thousands of details performed at the hands of scores of individuals. No general contractor can possibly oversee every one of these elements, and the very nature of human fallibility dictates that some mistakes and oversights will occur, even when the most talented and best-intentioned trades people are involved.

Buyers should let their builders know up front that they intend to have the work inspected by an independent third party construction expert to help set a tone with the builder and let them know that things must be done properly. Buyers should begin communication with the inspector as soon as the builder's contract is signed.

What Happens When the Inspection Report Cannot be Cleared?

The termite and pest inspection reports must be cleared or resolved prior to closing as normally required by the lender, but it is in the best interest of the buyer. If the report cannot be cleared prior to closing, any balance due the inspector will be held in an escrow account until both the buyer and seller sign off that the repairs have been completed to their satisfaction. As mentioned previously, many lenders will not release loan funds until the report has been cleared, meaning the parties may or may not be able to close until this issue has been resolved. If the buyer put an inspection clause in the purchase contract and repair issues cannot be resolved, they can back out of the deal assuming that the repairs exceed the repair cap that was also included with the clause (Review "Creating a Purchase Offer" in Chapter 2). The earnest money must be refunded. Another alternative is simply negotiating a lower price that will compensate for the needed repairs. When pursuing either alternative put your demands in writing. Send a copy to the seller, the seller's attorney, the seller's real estate agent, and the closing attorney or title agent.

Getting Insurance with Known Structural Problems

Some companies will insure a property with known structural problems. They simply write the problem area out of the policy. Getting this past the lender, however, will create another problem since most lenders do not want to close on a partially insured property with structure problems to boot.

Section 3.03: Surveys

A survey, sometimes called a plot plan, is a drawn map showing the locations of property boundaries, the locations of improvements, easements or rights of way, and encroachments. In addition, surveys reveal flood zones in the form of a flood plane report, certainly something of interest to prospective buyers.

An easement or right of way is the right of another person to use your land. There are various types of easements. For example; if a property is landlocked, the owner may have a right to use his neighbor's land to get to the nearest public road. This is called an "easement by necessity" or "driveway easement." It involves two parcels of land, the dominant tenement or parcel, which receives the benefit of the easement and the servient tenement or parcel, which has the burden of the easement. Be aware, the dominant tenement cannot just touch the servient tenement. It must abut enough to allow sufficient access of a vehicle to a public roadway. Otherwise, a secondary easement must be obtained. Another type of easement is the utility easement, which is the right of way an electric power company or telephone company has over your property to service the utility lines. A utility easement is beneficial to the property because most owners want electric and phone service. An easement generally runs with the land, meaning regardless of who owns the property the easement stays with the land. Thus if an owner sells a property, the buyer takes the title subject to the easement. *An easement is legally considered a separate piece of property unto itself. For this reason, it will require a separate title search.*

An encroachment is a structure that is placed or built on a public right-of-way with permission from the governing municipality. The municipality may authorize such encroachments by granting a license agreement. Encroachment information must appear on the deed.

A survey must show access. Access is the ability to get to a public roadway. If a property does not have access, the seller must secure an easement, probably the only option, before closing. In this event, the lender must be notified immediately as securing a private easement could significantly hold up the closing.

Lenders sometimes require surveys, but the buyer should order one as it is in his or her best interest. No one wants to buy a property only to discover it is substantially smaller than advertised or has an easement running through the front yard. Normally, the surveyor is selected by the buyer and is scheduled by either the buyer or the buyer's attorney. On average, a survey will cost between $500 and $650 to be paid for by the buyer.

The lack of a survey will require an exception on the "Lawyer's Certificate of Title" which is explained in more detail in Chapter 4, Section 4.02. Buyers will be faced with two survey fees. The first is for the actual survey and the second is for the title insurance company to check that a survey was done and that the property has clearly defined boundaries.

A buyer can save money by just requesting an "update" from a company that previously surveyed the land.

The surveyor should be given the following information:

- lender's name and address
- buyer's name as will appear on the deed and current address
- current owner's name and current address
- available legal description of the property and address
- name of the title insurance company
- date of closing or date the survey is needed
- where and to whom to send the invoice and copies of the survey
- number of required copies
- name of person to contact regarding problems with the survey

Geological Reports

Buyers in states that experience earthquakes will be required to obtain a geological report as part of the survey. It will reveal geological faults and the properties relationship to them. This assessment must be done by a geological firm.

Case Study: Eric Bozinny

This anecdote shows why surveys should be done before closing. Discovering geological problems after the sale can be costly.

We acquired our Queen Anne property back in January. If I were to do it all over again, I would have passed. However, we are stuck with a tear down that has massive water

Case Study: Eric Bozinny

issues. Literally rivers of water flow out of springs from the hill above and through the basement of the current structure. It was a mistake at the time to buy it because we were too new to get into this type of project. I tried working with a man who was recommended, but the fit wasn't right. I got as far as getting a survey done, and he wanted me to take the next step of bringing Geo Services in to do soil engineering and propose ways to manage the water. The price was $4,000 for that work so I looked for other options. Earlier this month, on the suggestion of a trusted agent, I got a second opinion from a sewer contractor she recommended. He knew right away there would be water problems because the street above our property that runs along the ridge of the hill is known for spring water flow

issues. Anyway, he said that it would be expensive, that well points would need to be placed deep into the soil. These are perforated tubes, screened on the bottom that allow water in the surround soil to collect, and thereby prevent any soil shifting. It will be expensive.

Section 3.04: Property Assessment or Appraisal

An appraisal will be scheduled by the lender, with the appraiser, an unbiased third party, having been selected by the lender as well. However, buyers can and should request an American Institute of Real Estate Appraisers Member, as they are the most qualified. The appraiser's fee, around $350, is paid by the buyer sometimes at closing and sometimes up front at the discretion of the lender. The appraisal itself is a valuation of the property, which must be done to ensure it has sufficient value to serve as collateral for the loan. Consequently, the appraiser's estimated value will always be the standard maximum amount allowed by the lender to be loaned out. As lenders will only allow 80 percent of the property's value to be borrowed, a $100,000 property can generate an $80,000 loan. Larger amounts must be borrowed with mortgage insurance or as a home equity line of credit. Clearly, the appraisal protects the lender, but it also protects the buyer, preventing them from getting into a property they cannot resell should hard times arise. Just for the record, bribing an appraiser is a federal felony offense that can earn jail time.

Section 3.05: Insurances

At this point, buyers should be arranging the insurance required by their lenders (refer to Chapter 1, Section 1.04). Because insurance costs can vary widely, buyers must take the time to shop around. Get an early start. One time-saving alternative is to secure an insurance agent who will shop multiple carriers for you. Unfortunately, these representatives can charge widely varying commission fees, leaving the buyer in the same predicament of needing to shop around but not to as great a degree.

After a policy has been selected, the buyer will need to sign the policy documents and pay the premium. Problematically, the policy cannot be put into effect until closing, leaving the purchaser in the awkward spot of frantically running all over town on closing day. To help with this, ask the carrier if they can accept payment over the phone and fax insurance certificates, promise of insurance. Ask your agent to obtain policy documents for your signature in advance. You may find that none of these options is available but inquiring will not hurt.

Section 3.06: Home Warranties

A home warranty is an insurance policy designed to cover general household repairs that usually costs $300 to $500 per year. A decent home warranty policy will cover the heating and cooling systems, the plumbing systems including major clogs, leaks, pumps, pipes, valves, and fixtures. They will cover major appliances even if they were purchased "as is." The electrical systems including the exhaust fans, general wiring, and garage door openers will be covered. However, policies will not cover rewiring required due to obsolescence. The same is true for the plumbing system. In other words, do not buy a building known to have out dated wiring and plan to have it replaced by the home warranty company. Be sure to read the policy. Most carriers will offer several versions for you to choose from, for other exclusions that could present a problem.

Sellers should consider purchasing a home warranty policy if the buyer does not do this for himself or herself. Although it involves a small expense, it could protect you from smaller lawsuits and discourage downward price bargaining. Additionally, the policy becomes effective immediately but does not have to be paid for until after closing. This means the seller could use it to fund repairs deemed necessary by the buyer before closing. This also means if your house sits on the market for a long time, you will not pay for repairs incurred during that time and still not pay the premium until the house sells. Frequently, the buyer's real estate company will offer to purchase warranty insurance out of his or her commission to protect themselves and the agency. Sellers should ask the agent if the company plans to do this.

There are many warranty companies, but American Home Shield (AHS) is currently the largest and has been in business for 35 years. Their Web site address is **http://www.ahswarranty.com**. I do not intend this as a sales pitch for AHS. It is just a place to start. There are many excellent companies to choose from. AHS provides 24-hour service seven days a week. Do not select a company that does not cover around the clock service because you will invariably have a problem at the most inconvenient time.

I will note here that one problem with home warranty companies is that they typically encourage policyholders to repair and not replace (causing a great deal of aggravation if the repairs become ongoing). They will insist on limping along even after the necessity of replacement has become obvious. My husband and I had this experience with our hot water heater, which we ultimately replaced on our own dime.

Section 3.07: The Last Days of Escrow

Unbeknownst to most new buyers, there will always be a multitude of last minute details to take care of before closing. This will happen no matter how experienced your representation or how well prepared you are. Plan to schedule vacation or personal days for at least the day before and the day of your closing. Although, you may want to just take vacation for the entire week and plan to begin moving the day after closing, which will also provide you with a cushion should something go wrong and you need to push back closing at the last minute.

Negotiating Through Problems

The Buyer's Perspective

The negotiation process will go like this: the buyer will present the inspection report, indicating which parts are unacceptable and threaten to make an exit if something is not done about it. The seller will take the position that the property is fine, but negotiate only because the buyer is insisting. The buyer will make demands. The seller will counter. Both parties will offer and counteroffer a number of times until a deal is reached or one party decides to withdraw.

Most buyers do use problems discovered during the inspection process to negotiate a lower sale price. They will have to make the repairs on their own dime or lose money trying to resell. A buyer should not take a hit for the seller. However, be selective about what you ask for. Requesting petty repairs could blow the deal but asking for major repairs is completely reasonable. What is the difference between a major and minor repair? If you need to make a repair before you resell for the same price you are being asked to pay, there is a problem and you should ask for a price reduction. As in the case study, unfinished renovations and faulty plumbing are legitimate issues to discuss with the seller. Moreover, not asking can lead to regrets later as the case study showed, especially when one major repair uncovers more problems. A buyer certainly takes this chance when they agree let things go.

Negotiating can go three ways; the seller agrees to do the repair, the seller agrees to reduce the sale price to compensate for the cost of the repair, or the seller seeks another buyer who is not as smart as you are. Having the seller handle the repair is the best option for two reasons. First, no one can look into the future to see exactly how much a repair will ultimately cost. Negotiating a lower sales price is fine as long as the repair does not cost twice what you expected. Second, one repair can sometimes uncover another needed repair, driving up the total cost. If you persuade the seller to fix the problem, require the use of a licensed contractor. Not doing so would be foolhardy because, of course, this person will be motivated to spend as little money as possible when fixing the problem. You will have saved nothing if you need to redo the repair after you take ownership.

Buyers who choose to accept a lower sale price in lieu of a repair accept the risk that one repair will reveal another needed repair or cost more than anticipated. Inspectors and professional licensed contractors can assess this risk. Do not hesitate to request a work estimate from an unbiased third party licensed contractor before agreeing to take the lower sale price option.

If you are facing major repairs and have negotiated from every angle, searched your brain for every compromise and tried bringing in an unbiased third party to no avail, you should consider backing out of the deal. As difficult as this may be to believe, some people are just looking to get something for nothing. No matter how much you love the property during escrow, you will likely only feel bitter and resentful when faced with thousands of dollars in repair bills later.

The Seller's Perspective

You are a well-meaning person and you just want to sell your house. Possibly, you need a larger house because your family is growing. Perhaps, you want a smaller house because your children are grown and you thought you could sink the extra money into your retirement fund. You lived in the house for some years and did general maintenance during that time. Everything seemed to be all right. Now you have discovered the house urgently needs a new roof only because your buyer just dumped a negative inspection report in front of you and is threatening to walk. How could you have known this? The roof looked fine from the ground. Sure, that one shingle had pulled up a little, but your neighbor nailed it down last year. You are now in the unfortunate position of needing to negotiate during escrow. You are certainly at a disadvantage, considering that putting the house back on the market may cause it to lose value when new buyers assume you are desperate to sell, which you very well may be, and will offer you less than the original buyer offered. To top things off, you now have to negotiate with a buyer who does not trust you.

Sellers should avoid putting their properties on the market "blind." Getting an inspection before listing a property will give you the advantage even if the inspection reveals needed repairs. If the property gets a clean report, great. If the property does not get a clean report, you can inform the buyer of needed repairs up front, making you the good person. Now you can negotiate a sale price with the buyer's trust.

Schedule Utilities

Contact utility companies and arrange to set up new accounts or make account transfers. Give them at least a week to complete this work. Plan to have some overlap of service for the moving day, but also in case your closing is moved back. Remember that at some times of the year, around the holidays for example, utility companies become short staffed as people take time away from work the same as any other business. Also, remember that many companies only provide emergency service on the weekends. Consider this and plan for it. Otherwise, you may find yourself staying in a hotel or delaying your move.

Utility Letters and Prorating Utilities

Sellers must arrange for their own utility account transfers. A kind gesture, on the seller's part, is to leave a little overlap of the essential utilities for the buyer, just in case they did not remember to make their own arrangements in a timely manner. Traditionally the buyer and seller will split the utility bills for the time the property was in escrow if it was empty. Otherwise, the 30-day cycle bills are prorated. The closing agent will handle this. If sellers want bills to be prorated, they should inform the closing agent of this in advance and bring their utility letters to the closing. This, of course, means you must arrange to have a copy before closing day.

Walk Through Inspection

Plan a walkthrough the day before closing, especially if the seller occupied the property during escrow. As mentioned in the previous case study, a lot can happen to a house in 30 days, like new pets that are not quite house broken. In addition to potential physical damage, look for items that are part of the sale but have been removed. If the property was vacant during escrow, look for theft, weather damage, and vandalism. Buyers should conduct this final walkthrough themselves and not ask the real estate agent to do it on their behalf. This purchase represents an enormous investment and asking another person to take the responsibility of double-checking it with so much at stake, leaving the agent open to a later lawsuit, is inappropriate. Most agents will not even do it if asked.

Loan Details and Appraisal

In most instances, the lender will call the buyer a few days before closing to schedule the completion of the mortgage. If this does not happen, take the initiative and check in. You do not want to miss your closing because the lender forgot about you. During the check in you should verify that the loan term, interest rate, origination fee, the loan amount, and any applicable points are the same as when you originally spoke. Verify that the interest rate will be fixed or adjustable whichever is applicable. Ask if there are any remaining issues to be resolved, if the lender has all of the information from you that he or she requires, and if you will need to sign any additional paperwork. Last, verify that the property was appraised, that the appraisal report was received, and that it appraised high enough to serve as collateral for the loan.

Borrowers will be required to sign an "affidavit of personal information," a legal document, requested by the lender, which attests to the accuracy of the personal information submitted by the borrower throughout the lending process. It is usually one of the last documents requested and is submitted with the loan application. Some lenders require payment of the loan origination fees before closing when the loan is actually started. You will want to inquire about this and arrange the payment if it is necessary.

After the mortgage process has been completed, borrowers sign the promissory note, sometimes done at the beginning of closing or at the office of the lender. However, it must be done before closing.

Property Insurance

Check in with your property insurance agents. Lenders will not allow the closing to go through without property insurance. You should receive your insurance binder containing the policy information several days before closing. Ask about it if it has not been received. Also verify that insurance certificates will be sent to the lender, that the agents know who the lender is and where to send the certificates (fax number or office location). As mentioned previously, buyers usually must obtain their policies immediately before closing. Ask for your last-minute instructions and payment and identification that you should plan to provide. Frequently, insurance agents have company-imposed rules regarding how premium payments can be received. For example, they might require that the premium be delivered to the office in person in the form of a check or cashier's check. Ask agents for these payment instructions. Otherwise, you may find yourself in an unexpected stressful situation of scrambling across town to deliver a check just hours before your closing.

Title Insurance

Title insurance is an insurance against loss should the title later be discovered to have problems such as unknown easements, encroachments, or inaccurate boundaries. There are two types of title insurance, lender's and owner's. Insurance required by the lender is lender's title insurance. The buyer pays for this insurance, but the lender arranges it. As mentioned, owners can secure their own title insurance. If you will be purchasing your own policy, you must let the closing agent know this several days in advance of the closing. The cost will vary depending on the amount of risk to be assumed. The following is a brief list of title agencies to get you started.

- American Guaranty Title Insurance Company
- Commonwealth Land Title Insurance Company
- Fidelity National Title Insurance Company
- First American Title Insurance Company
- Lawyers Title Insurance Corporation
- Old Republic National Title Insurance Company
- United General Title Insurance Company

Settlement Statement

Buyers should call the closing attorney or the closing agent and request a copy of the settlement statement the day before closing. Do not wait until the day of closing to realize your statement contains a gross error.

The closing statement is a breakdown of the fees to be paid upon settlement. A detailed explanation of the closing statement, sometimes called the settlement statement, can be found in Chapter 5, Section 5.02. The HUD Web site at **http://www.hud.gov/offices/hsg/sfh/res/rsphud1inst.pdf** also contains a line-by-line explanation of a generic closing statement.

Buyers should conduct a thorough review of fees to ensure they understand what will be charged and have an opportunity to contact the appropriate parties with questions. Contact the closing agent or attorney immediately if an error is discovered.

Other Pertinent Items

Call the sellers to remind them to bring keys to the property and other necessary information, such as appliance warranties, alarm codes, and garage door openers. You would be amazed at how often these items are forgotten.

Moving Plans

The moving checklist on the following page will help you avoid overlooking moving day details.

MOVING CHECKLIST

	Contact your insurance agent; transfer property, fire, auto and medical.
	Obtain insurance as advised by your lender.
	Get copies of your families' medical records or have them transferred.
	Obtain a lock box for your "impossible to replace" items or put them into a safety deposit box.
	Designate items will donate or sell, and dispose of them.
	Make the arrangements for your move. Start early. Purchase necessary supplies. Give yourself extra time to get boxes.
	Make your travel arrangements.
	If you hire movers, plan to be present for loading and unloading.
	Allow time for cleaning both properties. This includes freezer defrosting.
	Hire a babysitter.
	Arrange your change of address with the post office.
	Arrange to have the utilities transferred.
	Plan to begin packing early.
	Make arrangements to transfer your children to a new school.
	Plan meals and snacks for moving day.
	Pack your personal items, a first aid kit, and several changes of clothing.
	Have cash on moving day.
	Plan to pack some items at the last minute such as bedding.

chapter four

The Title and the Title Agent

Section 4.01: What is a Title Agent?

A Title agent is responsible for conducting the title search and issuing a certificate of title. In some states, an attorney must conduct the title search. Lenders always require these two things. Most title agents will issue title insurance to the lender and buyer with the cost of the search included into the policy premium. Sometimes they will conduct the closing, a requirement that varies by state.

Choosing a Title Agent and the Buyer's Rights

You will pay for the title search and have the right to choose the title agent. The seller does not have the legal right to name a title agent in the purchase agreement or to make choosing a certain agent a sale contingency. Doing so may be illegal. Your title agent may not require that you use a specific title insurance company or that you purchase their policy. Once again, doing so may be illegal. Your lender, on the other hand, may require the use of a certain escrow agent and title insurance company as a contingency of obtaining financing, assuming the two do not have a financial arrangement.

Section 4.02: The Title Search

A title is a document providing legal evidence of ownership of a land parcel. To transfer title is to transfer the ownership of the land it represents.

The title search is multiple tasks. First, information about the buyer and seller as well as the tax assessor's parcel number is collected to be made part of the community's public records after closing. This information will be used for future title searches.

Second, the agent will contact the assessors and tax collectors associated with the property and request records for taxes owed. The title search itself consists of collecting any applicable public records, deeds, promissory notes, liens, including any remaining unpaid mortgage for the property and wills and divorce settlements that may be connected to the property. This process can be labor intensive and require hours of phone calls in some cases, causing title searches to cost $300 to $400. Once gathered, all documents applicable to the title are reviewed for problems that will restrict the transfer and use of the title.

Last, a report of the findings is given to both the buyer and seller. Depending on your state laws, this report will have one of several names: a preliminary report, a commitment of title, or an encumbrance report. It provides the following information:

- Current owner's name

- Explanation of how the title is currently held

- Property address

- Taxes Due, and the date of the last tax assessment **Investigate the tax assessment records carefully. Grossly inaccurate tax records and the resulting inaccurate tax bills for more than five years can cause a foreclosure. Refer to the "Resolving Problems with a Title" section.

- Liens on the title

- Description of Title Restrictions (easements, rights of way, CC&Rs)

- Notification of *les pendens*

- Plat map, which is an overhead photo, a surveyors drawing or a computer generated drawing of the property with its dimensions

- Description of any conditions required by the title agent to issue title insurance

A certificate of title is given to the buyer, assuming the title is found to be clear. The certificate of title, a legal document, claims the current owner has the right to sell the property. If the title agent will be conducting closing, the closing documents are prepared at this point. Otherwise, they are prepared by a closing attorney.

Back Taxes

The title search will uncover back taxes owed. Buyers should note that many sellers, if the law will allow them to do so, will leave the previous 12 months' taxes unpaid with the intension of paying them out of the sale proceeds. If the title search reveals this, do not panic and assume the deal is blown. You were smart and put a perorations clause into your purchase agreement (refer to Chapter 2, Section 2.01). This clause states the date on which you become responsible for property taxes and that all bills are to be prorated in accordance to that date, protecting you from this bill.

Title Restrictions

A search of easements, right-of-ways, encumbrances, and Covenants, Conditions and Restrictions (CC&Rs) will be completed and the results reported to the prospective buyer. (For an explanation of easements and rights of way, refer to Chapter 3, Section 3.03.) The search consists of reviewing existing parcel maps maintained by the local municipality.

Encumbrances

An encumbrance is anything that will limit your use of the land. For instance, if another party holds mineral, timber, or water rights on the property, your use of the land cannot interfere with those rights.

Covenants, Conditions & Restrictions (CC&Rs)

The term CC&Rs, in reality, covers two classes of restrictions. The first class is restrictions put on a deed by the original land grantor, one of the subsequent owners or a homeowners or condominium association. These are referred to as private restrictions. Some examples are the prohibition of livestock, above ground swimming pools, or the storage of RVs on the property. The second class is public restrictions or those established by the local municipality, such as restricting the removal of sidewalks, the construction of a secondary structure, or opening a business in a residential zone. Frequently, these restrictions double as zoning codes.

CC&Rs grant reversionary rights or the right to repossess the real estate if they are violated. This is not a joke. Do not take the CC&Rs lightly. If you decide to raise cattle in a subdivision that prohibits livestock, for instance, the Homeowners Association can throw you out and take your land with the blessing of the courts. Buyers would do well to read the CC&Rs carefully and request clarification of anything they do not understand. As a warning, I had an associate with restrictions on indoor pets who thought she could flout the rules and get a macaw. Several months later, she tearfully found a new home for it. She thought the restriction of activities inside one's own home was excessive and never guessed she would be forced to part with her pet, but the Homeowners Association did uphold the restriction.

Zoning Certificates

Your title search will reveal how the property has been zoned. If this zoning does not suit your needs, you will need to apply for a zoning certificate, a legal document that changes the zoning only for your property without changing it for the entire community. In some cases a rezoning can be done at the court house or recorder's office. It involves completing the appropriate documents, submitting a proposal of your plans, and paying a fee. In other cases, you may have to present your case to the local zoning board.

Liens

Unpaid liens can create a problem because only a clear title can be transferred. Of course, any remaining unpaid mortgage for the purchase of the property itself does not affect the title transference because we assume that mortgage will be paid with the sale at closing.

There are four types of liens. The first is a property tax lien, a claim given precedent over all others that can cause a foreclosure if left unpaid for more than five years. The second type is a judgment lien which is the result of a lawsuit and a resulting court ordered monetary payment. These liens include judgments made on the behalf of a creditor. They can also take the form of a divorce decree for alimony payments that were not received or other divorce-related issues. Mechanic's liens filed by contractors for work done to the property are the third kind. Federal and state liens imposed for a failure to pay federal and state taxes or inheritance taxes are the fourth type.

Liens must be paid or refinanced with collateral other than the property, after which the title can be cleared by either a title agent or a real estate attorney. There is one exception. The title can be transferred if the buyer accepts the lien, meaning the buyer would become responsible for its repayment. The legal term for this action is "taking title subject to exceptions."

> **TIP**
>
> Unbeknownst to some sellers, liens can be home equity lines of credit. Sellers can sometimes innocently think these credit lines are part of the mortgage and, in fact, may have been created with the mortgage to cover closing costs, but they are separate liens. They must be paid or refinanced into the mortgage before a title can be transferred.

les pendens

les pendens is Latin for lawsuit pending, meaning exactly what one would assume: a lawsuit involving the property is pending.

When a lawsuit involving a property is pending, the owner is required to file a *les pendens*, containing a legal description of the property, with the local courthouse where the property title is held in record. Doing so serves to prevent its sale or refinancing. However, a seller is required to file a *les pendens* when facing foreclosure. This means that if you are purchasing a property from a creditor as the result of a foreclosure, you can expect to find a *les pendens*, which will not affect the sale. In fact, its presence is part of the sale. The creditor, at closing, will discharge the *les pendens*.

As a side note, property owners facing a suit against a property should not file a *les pendens* until the suit has been filed because should the suit be dropped, the *les pendens* will slander the title, diminishing its resale value. The same warning holds true for independent *les pendens* filers who could be sued for slander of title by the owners should the suit fail to be filed.

Adverse Possession

Adverse possession comes into play in this example. One party erected a fence 10 years ago that encroached into 15 feet of the others' property. The fence has remained undisputed all this time. Now the rightful owner wants the fence to be moved and the property returned. Because the fence remained for so long, the fence builder now owns that 15 feet of property. If you are told by the seller that the neighbor's fence is no big deal because it has been there for 10 or more years, seriously consider its position as that property might not be returned to you after the sale.

How is the Title Held?

This is an important question to be reviewed upon receipt of the title search report. For example, if the title is held in joint tenancy, meaning a group of tenants hold equal rights to the property, each of the tenants must be present at closing, not just the representative seller. Here is another example: if a divorced husband and wife hold the title as community property, both parties must be present at closing, although only one party represented the property as the seller. The seller may be a minor, whose trustor must agree to the sale and sign the closing documents. Go to section 4.05 for an explanation of the ways title can be held.

Abstract of Title

The escrow agent will order an abstract of title as one of his other responsibilities. It will be given to the buyer with the title search results. It is a record from the last time title insurance was issued all the way back to the property's first title or at least into the past 30 years. Most professionals recommend having it examined by an attorney. Know that your attorney may need to consult an expert if faced with arcane law, and that will incur a consulting fee.

Verifying the Title Search

After the title search has been received, buyers should walk through the property with the report in hand to verify its accuracy. You will compare the property to the plat map checking for things like encroachments of the city or your neighbors. Tiny issues such as your neighbor's dilapidated shed being located on your property because the boundaries were unclear can initiate fierce legal battles. I once worked for an attorney who defended in a two-year legal battle over the removal of a tree. The final bill was $30,000.

> **TIP**
>
> Be nosy! Why shouldn't you? You are about to pay a considerable sum for this property! Make your title report walkthrough and your final walkthrough unplanned. Your real estate agent will be able to give you access to the property. Go ahead and look around the property for potential problems that tenants did not disclose in the estoppel letter or repairs in progress that you were not informed of. While you are in the process of double-checking the title report, check your local zoning laws and buy knowing your limitations.

Resolving Problems with a Title

First, the title agent or attorney who performed the title search is the person to go to with questions or requests for assistance. If you are uncertain about the meaning or potential consequences of something revealed in the title search, also bring these questions to the title agent or attorney who is an independent third party — an unbiased resource with a pre-existing knowledge of the property's title and an understanding of the laws concerning holding and transferring title.

As mentioned previously, unpaid taxes are a common title problem as owners, knowing the property will be sold forthright sometimes will leave them unpaid, intending to pay them out of the sale proceeds. These bills must be paid at closing; otherwise, the title cannot be transferred.

Another common issue is creditor judgments mistakenly assigned to the seller because the real debtor has a similar or identical name. The title agent or attorney can resolve this by sending an affidavit, signed by the seller, attesting that he or she is not the debtor.

In some instances, the seller will not be aware of a lien. The title agent or attorney can usually request that the title be cleared with the condition that the debt is paid at or before closing. In the event the debt is to be paid at closing, the title agent or attorney will distribute these owed funds before the sale proceeds are passed to the seller.

The last common problems are tax discrepancies. The tax records and plot map do not match, meaning inaccurate tax bills were paid in the past. If the discrepancy is small, you will probably be able to work it out with the assistance of your title agent or attorney. However, if the difference is large and has been ongoing for more than five years, part of the property could be foreclosed or claimed and sold by the state.

To the buyer, do not panic. Your purchase contract calls for the conveyance of a marketable title and it included a disclosure clause, giving you an out.

Section 4.03: Certification of Title

Verifying Ownership and Certificate of Title

As mentioned previously, the title search will verify that the seller actually owns the property thus giving him or her legal right to sell it. Verification is done through a search of public records, wills, divorce decrees, and an evaluation of the deed itself. A consistent record, an abstract of title, must be established without breaks of each time the title was transferred. Then a certificate of title is issued and signed by the title agent. In most states, a search is required back to the root of title or to the last 30 years usually meaning back to an original quitclaim deed or warranty deed. Sometimes this extensive search can be circumvented by securing a buyer's title insurance policy that will allow a search of only the current transaction: the current seller to the current buyer. A thorough title search is in the buyer's best interest, but in cases where records have been lost or destroyed buyers may have no other option.

Attorney's Certificate of Title

If an attorney has conducted the title search, which is required in some states, the buyer will be issued an "Attorney's Certificate of Title." It is the same as a "Certificate of Title." In some cases the legal term used for this document is "Title Opinion."

"Title Commitment"

The "Commitment of Title" is a compilation of the findings from all of the searches done for you along with any exceptions to be put on your title insurance. It is usually called a preliminary report that comes from the title agent or the attorney who conducted the search. This report protects both the buyer and seller by creating a clear written understanding of the circumstances of the title prior to closing. It also comes with an "Affidavit of Title," signed by the person who conducted the search and attesting to the accuracy of the report.

Section 4.04: Title Insurance

Title insurance is very different from other insurance. While other insurers guard against unforeseen future events, title insurance protects against events that have already passed and are unknown today. Title insurers try to eliminate their risk by meticulously searching through title recorder's records, leaving no paper unchecked, but no one is perfect. Title insurance can be purchased for real property, an easement, or a life estate.

A life estate is formed by a joint tenancy title which will be explained in the next section. Besides owners' and lenders' policies, there is also a construction policy to be used exclusively for construction loans; however, its use is less common.

As previously mentioned, most title agents issue title insurance to the lender and buyer, with the cost of the search included in the policy premium. The policy protects the seller from a buyer's lawsuit and the buyer from monetary loss in the event the title is defective. Title insurance also protects against unknown liens inherited by the buyer without his or her knowledge.

In most instances, a title is defective because the governmental records were incorrect. Having a defective title could mean the land cannot be developed because another entity holds water or mineral rights or incorrect zoning information prevents the buyer from opening a new business. These are just two examples to help you understand that titles can be defective in many ways.

Section 4.05: Ways of Holding Title

Case Study: Chris Florko

Relationships are one factor preventing many people from purchasing real estate because they assume the risk of loss is greater within a partnership ownership than with sole ownership. In some instances, that assumption is true; however, you should not assume that is always the case. The following study describes how two unmarried people worked out their home ownership, followed by an explanation of ways to hold title.

Initially, I had more income to make a monthly mortgage payment, but she had the means to make a large down payment, which reduced our risk to the lender, thus reducing our interest rate. Ultimately, the reduced interest rate worked in our favor because now we can still pay the mortgage even if one of us were to lose our job. Several years into the mortgage, we both have good jobs and now split the monthly mortgage payment, which is great because splitting means we both have more spending money. She originally took the title as her sole and separate property because she had great credit, again helping with the interest rate. Later we changed it to community property, giving both of us the right to half.

Although we did not work things out this way, we considered the alternative of one person paying the mortgage and the other paying the utilities and incidental expenses.

Private Citizens

Joint Tenancy

Joint tenancy is sometimes called a concurrent estate or co-tenancy and is related to a section of property law that describes how people can own real estate together, called common law. In this case, tenant does not mean renter, but joint owner. Each jurisdiction is different, but most recognize three ways of holding property as a group. They are tenancy in common, joint tenancy with right of survivorship, and tenancy by the entirety. The main difference between joint tenancy and the others is right of survivorship. This means the other joint tenants automatically inherit the deceased tenant's portion regardless of the individual's will; they also inherit any property related debts. Besides right of survivorship, joint tenancy gives the titleholder the right to sell their part of the whole and to create debts without the consent of the others.

To create a joint tenancy all tenants must acquire the property at the same time, the titles must be identical and without differing restrictions, each party must have an equal share, and each tenant must have the right to possess the entire property. If one of these elements is missing, the title will default to a tenancy in common. The implication is that new owners who buy in cannot become joint tenants. They default in as tenants-in-common. Those buying into a joint tenancy must understand they will get a unique title that does not necessarily grant the same rights as those of the joint tenants. Also, they will not automatically inherit the joint tenants' portions.

When joint tenancy is established, each tenant is granted identical rights. They are unrestricted access, an equal portion of the profits, and owing an equal portion of the costs of ownership and maintenance. On the downside, tenants are not obligated to contribute to or participate in improvements even if these improvements increase the value of their investment.

Tenancy in Common

In a tenancy in common each person is a separate and distinct owner with a unique title. Each share of the property can be different. However, the shares are assumed identical unless the deed states otherwise. Owners need not take possession simultaneously. Owners can mortgage and create liens on their property, but these debts are separated from the other tenants and do not pass to the others upon that individual's death. Last, title can be passed through a will, and the other tenants will not automatically inherit the deceased tenant's portion. Meaning, if you want your heirs to inherit your property, set up a tenancy in common not a joint tenancy. When the title is broken, after the death of a tenant, the land must be divided in accordance to the portion given by each title and new individual titles created.

Tenancy by the Entirety

This type of title is available only to married couples and both people are treated like one owner entity. This title gives right of survivorship to each person, meaning if one person dies, ownership automatically passes to the other without probate. Creating a tenancy by the entirety has the same obligations as creating a joint tenancy; both tenants must acquire the property at the same time, the titles must be identical and without differing restrictions, each party must have an equal share, and each tenant must have the right to possess the entire property. In the event of a divorce, this title defaults to a tenancy in common.

Community Property

To hold a community property title one must live in a community property state. There are 10: Alaska, Arizona, California, Idaho, Louisiana, Nevada, New Mexico, Texas, Washington, and Wisconsin. It is usually established as the result of marriage or a gift and must be divided, typically in half, in the event of a divorce. Note, in some states property obtained while married is considered community property even without a community property deed. However, if one spouse can prove the property was brought into the marriage separately it may be deemed separate property by a court. This type of title allows right of survivorship without probate. However, in some states, the spouse will only inherit half the property with the remaining half passing to heirs unless the will specifically states otherwise. Each holder may sell or will his or her half to another party without the consent of the other. One last note, in some states a domestic partner has the same title rights as a spouse.

Holding a title as community property can give one spouse a capital gains tax benefit if it is sold after the death of the other. Right of survivorship differs from one state to another, with some state requiring probate.

Sole and Separate Property

Sole and separate property is just that, your property. No other person holds any interest in it. You own it 100 percent. Only an individual single person or a married person can hold title this way. In the case of a married person, the spouse must sign away his or her rights through a quitclaim deed; otherwise, it is automatically community property. This is sometimes called severalty. Of course, this is only applicable in community property states (Alaska, Arizona, California, Idaho, Louisiana, Nevada, New Mexico, Texas, Washington and Wisconsin).

Business Entities

When a trust or business holds title, the legal term to use is "vesting title" and not holding or owning title.

Corporation

A corporation is a separate entity unto itself that has ownership rights, like a person. Upon the creation of a corporation, property ownership can be granted to it, but the property is also part of the corporation. The same is true when an established corporation purchases property.

Partnership

Due to the Uniform Partnership Act, a partnership of two or more people can own property just like a corporation. The partnership owns the property as a separate entity, while the property partially makes up what the partnership is.

Limited Liability Companies (LLC)

An LLC is a legal entity unto itself, like the corporation. Each LLC will be different as each is defined by its operating agreement. As a separate legal entity, it does have the right to hold property. Like the corporation, property is both held by the LLC and makes up the LLC.

Trust

A trust consists of a trustee that can be one person or a business that holds property for another person or people, called grantees. The trust holds the deed and works to protect the interests of the grantees while managing all affairs regarding the property. Those benefiting from the trust are called beneficiaries. The grantees and beneficiaries can be the same people or person, but do not necessarily have to be.

A real estate investment trust (REIT) is a tax designation for a corporation that has invested in real estate to eliminate corporate income taxes. A REIT can be publicly or privately help and can be traded on the stock exchange.

Section 4.06: Helpful Definitions for Buyers and Sellers

Abandonment - Voluntary surrender of a property and its title.

Acre - 4,840 square yards. Because of alternative definitions of a yard, the exact size of an acre will vary especially concerning antiquated recorder's records.

Ad-valorem Tax - Another term for property tax that you may see when receiving the title report.

Argus - A financial analysis program used in the real estate industry. It is often used to determine the value of real estate, including property tax values.

Assign - To grant the right to purchase. For example, a corporation can arrange to purchase a piece of property and then assign the right of purchase to a subsidiary, who will purchase it secondarily from the corporation.

Capital Gain (tax) - A capital gain is the appreciation of property after it was purchased. Under the United States Tax Code's section 1222, if an individual sells a property for more than they paid for it, a capital gains tax is owed. Additionally, if inherited property is sold for more than the original purchaser paid for it, the inheritor must pay capital gains tax upon its sale. This tax must be paid when a property is sold after being inherited through a community title.

Conveyance - The act of transferring a title from one person to another.

Copyhold - This is a complex old legal term that basically means a copy of the deed was held by a manor's court. Copyholds were gradually eliminated during the 19th century until 1920s legislation finally eliminated them completely.

Deed - A deed is a legal document used to grant a right, not necessarily a property title. However, that is its best known use.

Documentary Tax Stamps - This is a state tax, in the forms of stamps, required when a title passes from one owner to another.

Due-on-Sale Clause - A clause in a loan or promissory note that stipulates the full balance is due upon sale or transfer of the title.

Eminent Domain - The compulsory purchase of a property by a municipality, giving it possession of the title.

Equitable Title/Equitable Conversion - A law that states an intending purchaser becomes a title holder when he or she signs a contract stating they will purchase the property at a later date.

Escrow Payment - The legal term for property taxes to be paid as part of the mortgage.

Estate - A term referring to not just one deed, but all of an individual's property; however, real estate refers to just property and personal estate refers to just goods.

Fee Simple/Free Hold - A general type of common law ownership under which the types of community property ownership fall. This is absolute ownership, but it is limited by the governmental powers of taxation, eminent domain, police power, and escheat. It can also be limited by encumbrances or restrictions on the deed. Escheat is the transference of land to the state in the event it has been left without an owner. For example, if an owner died without a will or heirs, the land would be absorbed by the state as an escheat.

Gramdan - A type of land grant in which an individual gives a land deed to a community for its benefit.

Grant Deed - A legal document that transfers ownership of property from one party to another. This is different from a quit claim deed that simply relinquishes ownership without granting new ownership.

Immovable Property - An obsolete term for real property.

Land Trust - A organization formed to hold a land deed and use the land in accordance with the organization's charter.

Leasehold - A individual or organization purchases a leasehold or the right to occupy land for a specific period of time without taking the deed. A typical leasehold time frame is 99 years.

Life Estate - Life Estates are straight forward, but the ways individuals use them are not. If the terms of the life estate are complex, you should have it reviewed by an attorney. The basic principal is that entity "A" will permit or sell the right to hold a deed to entity "B," but the right is only in effect during the life of entity "B." At the death of entity B the deed passes back to entity "A." However, entity "B" can sell the property to another party even though it will revert back to entity "A" upon entity "B's" death. In essence, life estates create a life long rental agreement and not a true transference of title.

Other Real Estate Owned - Other real estate owned is property repossessed and therefore owned by a lender. It is property "other" than that owned by the lender as part of its normal assets.

Periodic Tenancy - A tenant lease without a defined end date.

Tangible Property - Property that is real and can be touched.

Tax Participation Clause - A tenant lease clause indicating a tenant has agreed to pay all or part of the property taxes.

Tax Sale Certificate - This certificate is purchased at a tax sale and transfers the tax lien to the purchaser, resulting in tax payment to the municipality. The original debtor then pays the tax plus interest to the purchaser.

Tenement - Any solid property that can be owned such as land and buildings.

Tenure of Land - This term means the title and all the rights bestowed by the title go to the land owner and no one else.

Title - Legal document indicating the owner of land and the rights granted to that person with the ownership.

Title Guarantee Policy - As discussed in the text, this is a policy provided by a seller, who cannot produce a title abstract.

Transferable - A title that can be passed from seller to buyer.

Trust Deed Lien - Refer to Chapter 1, Section 1.03. A deed securing a loan.

Trustor - Refer to Chapter 1, section 1.03. A person who borrows money using a deed as collateral.

Warranty Deed - A type of deed in the which the seller makes guarantees to the buyer. Warranty Deeds are broken into two covenants or guarantees, present and future.

- Present Covenants:

    – Covenant of Seisin and Covenant of Right to Convey
    Seller promises he or she has the right to sell the property.

    – Covenant Against Encumbrances
    Seller promises the title has no encumbrances other than those disclosed.

- Future Covenants:

    – Covenant of Warranty and Covenant of Quiet Enjoyment
    Seller promises no one will claim to hold the title in the future.

    — Covenant of Further Assurances

    If the seller failed to pass a valid title, he or she will do whatever.

A great resource for an expansive list of real estate terms and definitions is *The Complete Dictionary of Real Estate Terms Explained Simply: What Smart Investors Need to Know* by Jeff Haden. This is an A-to-Z guide packed with over 2,400 terms. It is available from Atlantic Publishing Company (**www.atlantic-pub.com**, Item # CDR-01).

chapter five

The Closing

Section 5.01: Loose Ends to Tie up Immediately Before Closing

First-time real estate buyers especially should read Chapter 3, section 3.07 if they have jumped ahead instead of reading this book straight through. This section will provide valuable advice about what to expect and how to prepare as your escrow winds down, the busiest time of your property purchase.

Section 5.02: Closing Documents

Although the law does not specifically state it, the real estate transaction is completed when all documents have been signed and all transactions are finished at the closing. However, by the time the buyer and seller sit down at closing they are both legally bound to complete the transaction.

Closing Instructions

What does the process itself consist of? Just before closing, the closing agent will write out closing instructions. These are meticulous instructions detailing every transaction to take place at the closing. Each party will sign off on these instructions. However, there is not a prescribed legal format for them. In addition to meeting legal standards, these instructions must follow the guidelines set forth in the purchase contract and the requirements of the escrow agent.

Case Study: Nancy Spivey

Take the closing advice of this mortgage broker.

Closing attorneys usually move swiftly, handing you one long document after another to sign. They briefly describe the document and then point to the signature line while looking at you with a smile on their face waiting for you to sign. Even though the pace may feel fast and you may feel rushed to sign the documents without thoroughly reviewing them, do not hesitate to stop and read all documentation and contracts, asking questions of the closing attorney as necessary. It is better that you take your time and ask all questions up front rather than end up unhappy, confused, and frustrated after the closing when it is too late to make changes. If you will not be living at the property you are purchasing, be sure that the mailing address on closing documents is YOUR MAILING ADDRESS and not the property address. You do not want these important documents getting lost or being read by others. I once purchased an investment property from an estate where there were nine children and nine quit claim deeds. Unfortunately, all of the recorded deeds from the closing were lost when they were sent to the property address and never returned. It is much easier to make sure that your mailing address is correct than it is to get the deeds and other pertinent information after they have been lost. Be sure that a copy of the appraisal is included in your closing package.

This person will gather and prepare every legal document required to make the monetary and title transfers. These include conditions that must be met before escrow can close, a listing of items to be prorated, a statement of who pays which fees and authorization for the escrow agent to release held fees. Many agents now use computer programs to formulate the instructions because of their complexity.

The instructions can be bilateral or unilateral. That is, both parties can sign one copy or each party can sign their own copy. When unilateral instructions are used, the real estate agents will serve as go-betweens collecting information from both parties during the instruction formation.

After instructions have been signed, they are legally binding, and changing them will be difficult or even impossible. Therefore, one should check and be certain of all the totals being presented. Escrow will remain open until these instructions have been carried out.

<table>
<tr>
<td>TIP</td>
<td>Do not attempt to conceal information that should be included on the closing instructions. Give the closing agent a copy of your purchase contract. Your agent must have all pertinent information about your sale to make closing instructions that are legally binding. Therefore, withholding information will not help you. Bilateral closing instructions must be identical. Neither party can make changes to one copy and not the other; otherwise, the law will not hold that the instructions be followed.</td>
</tr>
</table>

Buyers and sellers can write their own closing instructions, but it is not recommended as it requires an in-depth understanding of real estate law. Remember these instructions are legally binding. However, if you choose to do this, they must be written, signed by both parties, and revocable upon mutual consent.

Preparing for Closing

Call your closing agent the day before and again the morning of your closing to ensure no additional information is needed and that the documents will be ready on time. Most agents will be responsible and will call you in the event of a problem. However, you do not want to discover upon arriving at closing that you were not informed of a problem.

What Happens at Closing?

At the closing itself, legal documents of ownership are passed from one party to the other along with the money owed from the seller to their lender, from the seller to the attorney and real estate agents and from the buyer to the seller, title agent, attorney, title insurance agent, and lender. Depending on the nature of the transaction, documents to be passed and signed vary from one transaction to another. If the buyer is financing the purchase, the closing will include a promissory note, a deed of trust, and a "truth in lending statement." What follows is a detailed explanation of the typical documents and transactions.

Section 5.03: The Closing Documents Explained

Payoff Letter for Mortgage

To remove a lien from a mortgage or to payoff a mortgage you must have a payoff letter from the lender or creditor which lists the exact amount needed to payoff the debt within a specified time. After this statement is received, a cashier's check will be sent by the escrow agent to pay off the debt and clear the title. After the debt has been paid, the appropriate party will complete legal documents to clear the title. The person to clear the title and the process varies by state. Refer to the state-by-state review for an explanation of the process in your state.

The Deed

The deed is the document that passes a title. To pass the title it must meet these criteria:

- It must contain names of both the buyer and seller in terms of grantor/seller and grantee/buyer. Oddly, only the grantor must sign and date it in the presence of a notary public to make the transfer.

- It must be passed with something called consideration; usually this is the purchase price. In other words, something must be given in exchange for the title. The law does not specifically state that this must be money. (Money is traditionally what is passed.) When property is given as a gift, a token $1 can be passed. If the buyer and seller wish to keep the purchase price confidential and out of public record, they can list $1 on the deed.

- This somewhat archaic piece of law states the deed must be physically given to the buyer. This is usually done at the closing.

Affidavit of Title and Other Affidavits

The "affidavit of title" is a legal document equivalent to swearing an oath. It must be signed by the seller, who promises the title is clear and can be passed to the buyer. Other affidavits may be presented at closing. For example, sellers of inherited property may sign an affidavit swearing the real estate is their rightful property. Each one should be read — they tend to be short — and understood. One of the most important pieces of advice I can give is do not sign anything you do not understand.

American Land Title Association Statement (ALTA)

Much like the "affidavit of title," the ALTA Statement conveys promises from the seller to the buyer regarding the title. Among them are lack of easements, encroachments, and restrictions other than those previously disclosed. Unlike the Affidavit of Title, the ALTA Statement must be signed by both the buyer and seller. Moreover, signing this statement by both parties is a condition of the title insurance.

Trustee's American Land Title Association Statement (ALTA)

As the trustee is the one who holds a property for another person, a trustee must, like a normal seller, sign an ALTA promising the title is free from easements, encroachments, and restrictions other than those previously disclosed.

Promissory Note and Deed of Trust

These documents make up your legal promise to pay; therefore, you must check the loan amount, interest rate, monthly payment amount, and terms of repayment carefully.

Truth in Lending Statement

The "truth in lending statement" also known as the Regulation Z form is a statement of estimated loan fees that lenders must provide to you within three days of initiating a loan. It is an itemization of the fees you will be charged for taking out the loan, including fees to be charged later during the life of the loan. Most important, it discloses your annual percentage rate and points. (See Chapter 1, section 1.04.)

Right of Rescission Notice

This document is only provided to those who are refinancing an existing loan and intend to use the property as a primary residence. It provides the borrower an opportunity to back out within three days of initiating the refinance. Most lenders ask borrowers to sign this document twice. One request is made when the loan is started, and another is made three days later.

Fire Insurance Form

Signing this statement means you agree to the lender's insurance requirements, including the required types of coverage and the coverage amounts. Frequently, the lender will demand that you pay one year's premium in advance at closing.

Trustee Pay Proceeds Letter

Called a letter, but really more of an affidavit, this letter states that the trustor promises to pay the proceeds of the sale to the benefactor. The amounts to be paid, the payee, and the trust number are spelled out in the letter. In this explanation, I am referring to a trustor who manages a property and not a trustor as a creditor foreclosing on the property.

Closing Statement

The closing statement shows what will be paid by both the buyer and seller. Unlike the "truth in lending statement," it does not give estimates, but real figures. Knowing this, review the statement carefully as typos are hazardous to your bank account.

Housing and Urban Development (HUD) Settlement Statement

All closings include a settlement statement, but HUD requires that their own statement, called the HUD-1 form, be used. This is a statement of all monetary exchanges to be made at the closing and is required by the Real Estate Settlement Act of 1974. It must be given to the buyer along with a booklet called "Buying Your Home: Settlement Costs and Information" within three days of finalizing the loan. Every person involved in the monetary transaction must be given a copy of the HUD-1 form. However, the HUD-1 form is not required for purchases of 25 acres or more, vacant lots, and mortgage assumption purchases.

The items on the HUD-1 form are broken down into three categories: tax deductible in the current year, capitalized and added into the principal, and neither, meaning the fee does not fit into either of the two previous categories. Tax-deductible items are interest and points, the loan origination fee, and property taxes. Also, if the borrower incurs a pre-payment penalty by paying off the loan early, the pre-payment penalty is tax deductible in the year it is incurred. Title insurance premiums, attorney's fees, appraisal fees, recording fees, notary fees, escrow fees including the termite inspection fee, transfer tax, and the ALTA inspection fee are capitalized into the principal. Fire insurance premiums, mortgage insurance, and money put into impound accounts fall into the neither category.

Pre-Paid Interest

This is the interest due on the property loan from the date of closing to the first day of the next month. It is usually listed on the closing statement and paid at closing.

Bill of Sale

A bill of sale, like a store receipt, covers movable items to be included with the property such as furniture and outdoor fountains. The bill of sale will cover anything to be included with the sale that is not physically attached to the property. Besides this function, it closes the deal. This is the buyer's receipt for the purchase of the property.

Section 5.04: An Explanation of Selected Closing Statement Fees

Courier Fee

Some closing agents use a courier service to transfer documents such as insurance certificates when tying up the closing. If so, you will see the courier fees on the closing statement. Before you become upset about the fee, which can be high, remember that in some instances a courier must be used to complete the closing on time. Missing your closing deadline would cost much more.

Discount

If your loan has been discounted, you will not get the entire principal. This is done to compensate for a difference between what other investments are offering and what the lender can make from your loan. For example, if you borrow $100,000 with 2 points, you will receive $98,000. The lender will keep $2,000.

Discounts allow lenders to offer lower interest rates during a high interest rate market. It creates the appearance that borrowers are getting a better deal, and they may be; but do the amortization calculations, comparing lender's offers before jumping into a discounted loan. This practice began in the 1950s. Its use tends to come and go depending on interest rates.

Document Preparation Fee

Some closings require up to 50 documents that a paid employee must prepare for you. In most cases, the cost will be passed to the buyer. However, many lenders charge for the preparation of their own loan documents. This is ridiculous and a symptom of the lender's own internal bureaucracy problems. Buyers should take this up with their lenders.

Escrow Waiver Fee

Those borrowing more than 80 percent of the value of their property must put taxes due into an escrow account each month. Sometimes an impound account is used instead. However, a borrower can pay down the principal before closing negating the need for this escrow account. If a borrower does so, the lender may charge a fee for having opened the account. In some cases this fee is unfounded, and in others it reflects fees incurred by the lender as the result of your plan change. Unfortunately, borrowers may be unable to determine which the case is. However, taking the time to negotiate this point takes only a little time and could create a substantial savings for you.

First-Year Insurance

Many lenders require that insurance policies be paid one year in advance to assure that the policy will be maintained while business is sorted out, should the property be destroyed.

Flood Certification Fee

This fee pays the person who checked the flood status of the property: someone checked existing plat maps to see if the property is on a flood plane.

Impound Fee

If more than 80 percent of the property value is being borrowed, taxes will be collected with the monthly loan payment. The money is put into an impound account where it is held until the tax is due. An impound fee is a charge for setting up the impound account.

Judgment Payoffs

Normally judgment payoffs are only applicable to a seller or someone refinancing. Occasionally, a buyer's unpaid judgment debt will be discovered. In these instances, the buyer must pay off the debt before their lender can disburse the loan funds.

Lender's Legal Fees

Lenders who enlist the services of an attorney will pass the charges on to the borrower.

Discount Fee

A discount fee is incurred when a borrower has made a pre-existing arrangement to pay down the points assigned to their loan. Borrowers will always know about this fee in advance of the closing because it represents an arrangement made between the lender and borrower. If this fee appears on the closing statement and the borrower has not previously discussed it with lender, there is a problem. Check for mistakes on the part of the closing agent. Otherwise, the lender should be contacted right away.

Escrow Fee

As part of the purchase contract, the buyer's earnest money is put into an escrow account. A fee is assessed at closing for opening and maintaining this account.

Loan Lock-in Fee

Borrowers who chose to lock in their interest rates during prequalification may be charged a lock-in fee, created to offset the lender's loss when interest rates increase after the lock in. The fee is usually a quarter of a point and is due at closing.

Loan Payoff

A seller who owes money in the form of a loan on the property to be sold must pay off this debt at closing. The seller's lender will send information about the money owed and any payoff penalties to the escrow agent. The amount due is calculated based on the scheduled closing date. The amount due will appear on the closing statement as being owed by the seller.

Nonrecurring Costs (NRCC)

Some closing agents will lump together several fees under the "nonrecurring costs" heading. The costs are one-time charges. Examples are termite inspection and home inspection fees.

Photo Fee

A property may have been photographed several times during the sale process. Initially, it may be photographed for the sale listing. Appraisers sometimes require photos. The insurance agent will usually require photos as part of the policy. This fee is usually either charged to the buyer or split between the buyer and seller.

Settlement or Closing Fee

This charge might cover a lender's escrow account; however, in some cases it is a charge for closing documents. It is equivalent to being charged for a sales receipt. In this case, the borrower should make every effort to negotiate this fee with the lender.

Tax Service Fee

If you do not make your tax payments on time, your lender will pay them for you to protect their interest in the property. You will be billed later with added penalties. These penalties are known as tax service fees. Of course, foreclosure will begin after this bill is left unpaid. Buyers are informed of tax service fees at closing.

Termite and Fungus Clearance Fee

This is a charge from the pest inspection service for a certificate stating the property is clear. Lenders will not disburse funds without this certificate. Some states have their own form to be completed and included with the closing documents.

Termite and Fungus Work Fee

The termite and fungus work fee is charged for the service of ridding premises of an infestation. After the work is complete, a certificate stating the property is free of infestation is submitted to the closing agent. The fee for this service is normally paid at closing and appears on the closing statement.

Underwriting Fee

Fannie Mae and Freddie Mac borrowers may receive a conforming loan. This means after the loan has been processed it will be sold to either Fannie Mae or Freddie Mac. To ensure the sale will go through, the lender will submit the loan documents to these agencies. The agencies will review your loan and may ask you to change it or conform it in some way. For example, you may be asked to increase your down payment or show additional collateral. Your lender is the underwriter. Expenses incurred by the underwriter, your lender, such as processing additional paperwork to ensure the loan will be purchased are passed to the borrower as an underwriting fee.

Warehousing Fee

Lenders circulate their money as much as possible. By circulate I mean they keep it invested and earning money. The majority of their money is not present at the lender's building unless it is about to be used. Before the borrower closes, the lender will pull back the money to cover the loan. In the days before electronic transfers, lenders needed to store the money in a vault on the premises, unnecessary in modern times, but the term "warehousing fee" remains. This fee covers interest lost between the time the money is removed from circulation and the time it is loaned out to the buyer as well as costs associated with moving the money.

Wire Transfer Fee

If the borrower's loan funds must be wired or if the buyer's closing costs are wired, a wire transfer fee will appear on the closing statement.

Agency or Transaction Fee

Due to the competitive nature of real estate, many real estate agencies must give the agent a large portion of the commission to secure quality employees. Many agencies have been forced to give as much as 80 percent to the agent, leaving them without enough to cover office expenses. To counter this they have begun adding an agency or transaction fee onto the sale. This fee goes directly to the real estate agent's office. Even if the agent did not mention this fee when hired, you are obligated to pay it.

Yield Spread Fee

A borrower should never pay a yield spread fee. This fee is assessed when interest rates increase after a lock. This is the lender's effort to regain some of the loss. Charging this fee counteracts the lock. Why would a borrower request a lock only to pay this fee at closing?

Section 5.05: Last Minute Closing Questions

What Happens if You Decide Not to Sign a Document at Closing?

The decision not to sign a document, although the right decision in some cases should be considered carefully. Not signing, causing the deal not to close will probably result in bills from the mortgage broker or bank, the attorney, the closing agent, and the escrow agent for services not performed. Additionally, the seller may retain the earnest money and sue if the property sells for less after returning to the market. Sellers who refuse to sign could be liable for home and termite inspection fees as well as fees incurred by the buyer for services not received. This is not to imply one should feel pressured into signing. If you are faced with a mistake or misunderstanding that will cost you considerably in the future, obviously you should not sign. In most cases, if the closing agent or lender has made a mistake on the closing documents, it will be corrected quickly, and your closing will get back on track so long as everyone involved is informed of the problem and the steps being taken to resolve it.

If your lender's fees are excessive when compared to the truth in lending estimates, you may be stuck. One thing to consider is how much not signing will cost compared to the fees being imposed. Your closing agent will probably want to remain a neutral third party, appropriate although understandably frustrating. This is a good time to contact an attorney for professional legal advice.

How Should I Pay Closing Costs?

You are about to exchange a large sum. Think safety. You want evidence of your payment should a mistake occur. Therefore, cash payments are not recommended and may not even be accepted. A personal check may or may not be accepted by your closing agent as he or she cannot prove the availability of funds and must wait for them to clear—for an entire week. A cashier's check that will only take one or two days to clear or an instantaneous wire transfer is best. However, checking with the closing agent and going with his or her preferred payment is your very best option.

When Will Escrow Finally be Closed?

After the loan documents are signed, they must be processed through the lender's bureaucratic system, which should not take more than 48 hours. Your escrow will close by the end of the following day. After the loan has cleared, the money must be divided out to those owed. Last, the deed transfer must be recorded. These actions signal the end of the sale.

When planning the move in, keep in mind that bank holidays can delay your closing. Also banks may be closed for several days around a holiday. This heavy load may cause delays for you. A smart buyer will plan for a little overlap between residences.

Section 5.06: Proration and Fees to be Prorated

Understanding the System

A closing statement might be a little confusing for the uninitiated. The following is a guide to the basics. Debits are what you owe. You will be charged this amount at closing. Credits represent money owed to you. This money will be paid to you after closing from the escrow agent. The buyer and seller each have their own debits and credits. Proration is the dividing of a debit or credit.

Prorating is simple. Charges to be prorated are incurred prior to the sale that cover a period extending after the sale. Examples of items to be prorated are property taxes, rent, and condominium maintenance charges. To be fair, one party should not pay for charges covering a period when the other party will be in possession of the property. Proration fees paid in advance by the seller become credits to the seller. Fees paid by the buyer after the sale necessitates a credit due to the buyer.

Perorations are normally based on a 30-day period. When doing the calculation, you need to know the dates to prorate to and from. First, the amount due is divided by 30. The amount to be paid by each party is calculated by finding the number of days out of that 30 the buyer or seller had possession of the property. For example, if you are prorating from January 1 to January 30 and the seller owned the property from the first to the ninth, you would divide the total bill by 30. Then you would multiply it by nine. This calculation generates the seller's portion. The remaining is the buyer's portion. Here is another example using the same scenario. If real estate taxes are $100, you must divide $100 by 30 days giving you $3.33. Next, multiply $3.33 by nine days to get $29.97. The seller's portion of the tax is $29.97. The buyer owes the remaining $70.03.

Property taxes are assessed on a yearly basis, but may be due twice a year. If the property is sold during one of these two halves, remember, the seller will have owned the property for part of this six-month period. The buyer will own it for the other part of the six-month period. Therefore, a proration is required. To prorate is to split the six-month bill according to how many days of the six-month period each person had or will have possession of the property. The closing agent makes this calculation and fills in the total owed by each party on the closing statement.

Loan Payoff Interest

This is a seller's charge. Loan interest is paid in arrears. This means it is paid after it was due from the previous month. Because interest is paid in arrears, some interest will be due for the time between the last monthly payment and closing. It is prorated. For example, if the closing date is the 20th, the seller will owe 20 days of interest.

Section 5.07: Transfer Tax

Calculating Transfer Tax and Transfer Tax Declaration

The tax is a flat percentage of the sale price. It can vary a great deal, but an escrow agent can tell you what it is for a specific area. A guide to the transfer taxes levied in your state can be found in the State by State Review section. This tax is always listed on the closing statement. Transfer tax is assessed on the value of the property being exchanged. It is collected and paid by the escrow agent. It is paid by the buyer and can be levied in several forms. It is most commonly paid at closing. However, in some areas it is paid in the form of stamps or a supplemental tax. When the transfer tax is paid a "transfer tax declaration" is filed with the recorder's office by the closing agent.

County, City, or State Tax Stamp

Some municipalities tax the transfer of property with the tax represented as a stamp. The stamps are purchased by the buyer and attached to the deed. The fees are not usually very high, and the closing agent should secure the stamps for you. The cost of the stamps will appear on the closing statement.

Supplemental Tax

In some states, real estate is taxed when it is sold. However, the tax is assessed long after closing. If this is the case, a notice of the impending tax will appear on the closing statement. The tax is not paid at closing and its appearance on the closing statement only serves as a notice of a future bill.

Section 5.08: Leases

As mentioned previously in the text, leases are transferred at closing. The buyer should have been provided with an estoppel letter at this point. Refer to Chapter 2, Section 2.02 for an explanation of estoppel letters.

Assignment of Leases and Contracts

Any leases and contracts that come with the property, which the buyer has previously agreed to accept, are transferred at closing through an assignment of lease or an assignment of contract document. Of course, a copy of the original lease or contract should be provided. Buyers should have requested an estoppel letter to cover lease agreements. If this has not already been received, it must be provided at closing.

Security deposits are passed to the new owner in full. However, rents are prorated. Refer to the explanation of proration above. The security deposits and prorated rents must be listed on the closing statement.

Section 5.09: Affidavits and Required Legal Documentation

Grantor/Grantee Affidavits

A grantor is a person from whom a grant is made or a trust is set up. The grantee is the recipient. If your closing involves establishing a trust or grant land, the grantor and grantee need to sign affidavits which vary with their purpose. For example, if real estate is subdivided for another family member, the grantor and grantee will sign a "grantor's affidavit of family exempt subdivisions," a promise to not allow ownership to leave their family.

Warranty Deed

The definition of a warranty is, for example, if I have a warranty on a toaster, I can return or exchange the toaster should it break while it is under warranty. A warranty deed is similar. It is a warranty provided by the title insurance carrier, a promise that the buyer's title to a parcel of land will be defended should his or her ownership rights be questioned after the sale.

"Affidavit of Heirship"

An "affidavit of heirship" is exactly what it sounds like. It is a promise made by the heir of property that he or she is the rightful heir.

Death Certificate

When an inherited property is sold or when a property whose title was held in common is sold, an original death certificate will be required at the closing. Original death certificates can be acquired at the court house or recorder's office. Today they can be researched and ordered at a number of Internet sites.

Joint Tenancy Affidavit and Deceased Joint Tenancy Affidavit

A joint tenancy affidavit or a deceased joint tenancy affidavit is a legal document to be signed at closing by the joint tenancy title holders. It protects the buyer by providing a promise that the title is held in joint tenancy or was held by a now deceased party in joint tenancy.

Documents to Establish Identity

Buyers and sellers will be asked to present two forms of personal identification at closing. The usual list of widely accepted identification documents applies here. Accepted identification documents include a driver's license, a state issued photo identification card, a military identification card, or a passport. These photo identifications can be used in conjunction with a non-photo identification such as a birth certificate or social security card. Some businesses accept non-standard identification such as college or business identification cards, public library cards, credit cards, or car insurance cards. However, you should call the closing agent in advance to verify that these documents will be accepted.

Section 5.10: Taking Possession of the Property

The buyer takes possession in accordance with the terms laid out by the purchase contract. Legally, possession can be taken from the time the purchase contract is signed up to six months after closing. Buyers have no legal reason to want to take possession early. Any decision to do so should be for personal reasons.

Possession is normally assumed when the buyer is given keys. Keys are typically passed by way of real estate agents. If the purchase contract states possession is to be given at close of escrow, the keys are given after the deed transfer is recorded. If the purchase states as such, the agent cannot give the keys earlier without risking being held liable should the deed erroneously fail to be recorded.

Nothing prohibits taking possession during escrow. Sometimes it may be necessary to do so. For example, if the buyer is being transferred, he or she might need to move in immediately. In these situations, the buyer and seller can work out a lease. The buyer will become a renter until he or she takes possession.

The more likely scenario will be that the seller will want to retain possession after closing. A child in school is a typical reason. Once again, a lease should be arranged and the seller becomes a renter after closing. Smart buyers limit the length of their stay within the lease. Otherwise, nothing will prevent their stay from dragging on long after it becomes inconvenient. When agreeing to let the seller stay, keep in mind that sellers who refuse to leave in a timely manner may eventually need to be evicted, a costly development.

chapter six

Buying and Selling Under Special Circumstances

Owner financing is becoming increasingly popular. The interest rates of 2004 and 2005 were lower than we had previously experienced, meaning many buyers found it attractive to assume a seller's mortgage or obtain financing from the seller. The following explanations will be helpful to those wishing to pursue these options. However, both parties should enlist the services of an attorney before pursuing either of these options.

Section 6.01: Due on Sale Clause

This clause means if the owner sells or transfers ownership of his or her portion of a property, the entire note will be due upon closing, meaning the lender will honor the loan held only by the original borrower. Another party cannot assume it. The lender has every right to make this demand. After all, the lender has evaluated the original borrower's risk and formed the loan deal with the original borrower. This clause is sometimes called an acceleration clause because it moves the due date nearer.

Section 6.02: Assumptions

An assumption is created when a buyer takes over the seller's loan with the title transfer. Much of the time buyers can purchase this way without any money down. It is much like a credit card transfer with the debt simply being moved from one owner to another, frequently an alternative because while mortgages are normally 15 to 30 years, the average ownership is only five to seven years. If the seller's interest rate is lower than the buyer's would be, an assumption is a smart way to go. It can also allow buyers to avoid some closing costs.

Lenders have the right to and usually do charge an assumption fee. They can also raise the interest rate if the lender agrees to allow the assumption in spite of a due on sale clause. If the loan has a due on sale clause, the loan can only be assumed with the permission of the lender.

The loan is transferred at closing. A good closing agent will understand the process and be able to walk you through it. The buyer must sign an assumption agreement for the lender. A record of assumption of liability is logged at the recorder's office. The buyer will usually get a 30-day grace period, as is the case with a new mortgage. The original borrower is not connected with the loan after closing and does not maintain any liability, because a substitution of liability is recorded.

Is My Loan Assumable?

If the loan contains a due on sale clause, it is not assumable as stated in the previous paragraph. However, owners should read the entire clause as some will provide exceptions under which the loan can be assumed. The due on sale clause is not enforceable in some states. If the lender is in a due on sale clause state, but the property is not, the due on sale clause is void. However, before you jump for joy, know that the due on sale clause is enforceable in a non-due on sale clause state if the lender is a federal savings and loan. Further, if the loan originated before October 15, 1982, the clause is enforceable even in a state that does not honor it.

Section 6.03: Subject to Financing

Subject to financing means the buyer will take over the seller's loan, but the loan does not transfer. It remains in the seller's name. The buyer does not make any agreements with the lender. However, the buyer does receive a grant deed. The ultimate responsibility of the loan is still held by the seller. The seller and buyer will have formed an agreement between themselves, but no agreement will be made with the lender. A substitution of liability is not recorded. This type of transfer means the buyer is guaranteed to get the seller's interest rate. The down side is the buyer must produce cash to reimburse the seller for the part of the loan he or she has already paid. Of course, the buyer can take out an additional loan. A subject-to-financing transfer can only take place if the loan does not have a due on sale clause. Both parties are free to risk that the lender will not get wise to the transfer. This is a substantial risk considering the lender will have every legal right to demand payment in full, which could result in a bankruptcy in a worst case scenario.

Section 6.04: Wraparound Loans

Wraparound loans are essentially seller financing. They become popular when high interest rates create a buyers' market and when loan funds dry up in a poor economy. Here is a basic explanation. If a buyer cannot get financing, but the seller very much wants to move his or her property, the seller can let the buyer do subject-to financing. However, there is the problem of money already paid toward the seller's loan by the seller and the property's gaining value since its purchase. To compensate for these two issues, the seller will loan the buyer additional money. The two parties agree to the term and interest rate and form a legal agreement for repayment.

Here is more of a real life example of a wraparound loan. A seller purchased a property for $175,000 five years ago. Now he or she has listed it for $200,000 because $25,000 represents the equity the property has gained. Currently, the seller owes $150,000 on the property's mortgage loan. The buyer has $20,000 in available funds to use as a down payment. The buyer takes on the seller's remaining

$150,000 mortgage as a subject-to-financing. However, the buyer still owes the seller $30,000. When we subtract the $150,000 mortgage loan that the buyer will take from the $200,000 asking price, $50,000 remains. The buyer has $20,000 to put down, which leaves $30,000 of the $50,000 remaining. The seller lends the buyer this remaining $30,000. Remember that the property had gained $25,000 in equity since the seller originally purchased it? The buyer has given the seller his or her equity with the $20,000 down payment. The remaining $5,000 of equity is recouped with interest when the buyer repays the $30,000 loan to the seller. The seller will pay income taxes on the buyer's $20,000 down payment, but will stretch out the income tax due on the remaining $5,000 over the course of the loan he or she made to the buyer. If the seller had wanted to pay even less tax during the year of the sale, he or she could have taken less down payment from the buyer and made a larger loan.

The original loan remains in the seller's name, as is the case with a normal subject to financing situation. Wraparound loans can benefit sellers by helping them avoid paying tax on the sale of their property while allowing them to remove its equity.

Because wraparound loans reduce lenders' opportunities to make money, the legality of this type of financing has been challenged. Initially it was challenged in Wellenkemp v. Bank of America. Bank of America lost on the grounds that the lender does not have the right to recall an assumed loan unless the buyer's credit is substantially worse than the original borrower's credit. The legality of wraparound loans was challenged again after Wellenkemp v. Bank of America, leaving the situation in limbo. Later, Congress passed the Garner Bill, which made due-on-sale clauses enforceable on wraparound loans in all cases. However, wraparound loans formed before the signing of the bill, October 15, 1982, are exempt. The bill also includes the following exceptions: the transfer to a joint tenant after the death of another joint tenant, transference to an heir, transference as the result of a divorce settlement, and transference within a trust in which the borrower and beneficiary are the same person. The bill also allowed a three-year window of exemption for wraparound loans that were in formation when the bill was passed.

Section 6.05: Deed of Trust or Trustees Deed

As explained previously in this book, a deed of trust is a property deed used as collateral for a loan. Usually the loan will be used to acquire the same property held in the deed of trust which allows the lender to foreclose should the borrower fail to pay. In the event the lender is the seller, the seller retains the right to foreclose.

Section 6.06: Ownership Through a Trust

When an independent third party holds the deed of trust, the third party is called a "trustee for the beneficiary." Of course, the beneficiary is the rightful owner. This situation may be set up if the rightful owner is a minor or is unable to manage his or her own affairs for some reason. Why would you as an owner want to set up a trust when purchasing real estate?

- To hold assets for your heirs upon your death.

- To control the spending of the trust's beneficiaries.

- For the professional management of a real estate investment while you are living as part of retirement planning.

- To protect the beneficiary's assets in the event of a divorce.

- To protect the beneficiary's assets from creditors.

- To finance a child or grandchild's education.

- To protect your assets should you become unable to manage them.

- To minimize estate and income taxes.

- To avoid probate.

- To maintain privacy from everyone except the trustor and beneficiary.

Types of Trusts

Living Trust

A living trust is created for a living person during his or her lifetime. It facilitates the professional management of one's assets. Doing so can leave the beneficiary free to focus on other things such as travelling during retirement. There are two types: revocable and irrevocable. Revocable trusts can be changed or even ended during the holder's lifetime. Irrevocable trusts are the opposite.

Testamentary Trust/Trust Under Will

This type of trust is formed in a will and is irrevocable. The trust becomes active upon the death of its maker. It can be given to an individual or charity and can be used to minimize federal estate taxes by reducing the amount of an individual's estate eligible to be taxed. Various types of a testamentary trust can be formed such as an educational trust.

Children's Trust

This trust is sometimes referred to as a 2503(c) Minor's Trust after the section of the Internal Revenue Code upon which it is based. It provides you with the opportunity to minimize taxes on gifts you make to your children or grandchildren. This asset can be controlled until the minor reaches the age of 21. Because it is a gift, it is not part of the grantor's estate and not subject to estate taxes.

Who Can Be a Trustee?

A good trustee will be state chartered and regulated as well as FDIC insured. This means the trustee will be routinely examined by the state to ensure the rules and regulations applicable to a trust company are being adhered to, ensuring the safety of your assets. A state regulated trust will be compelled to hold insurance for it and to bond its employees. Because the assets will be the legal property of the client, should the company cease to exist, your assets will not be affected or subject to liquidation by creditors.

What is the Role of the Trustee?

A trustee will advise you in estate planning, make suggestions, and present you with solutions to your problems. He or she may or may not be an attorney, but should be able to refer you to one to implement your estate planning. Of course, individuals can do their own estate planning, and trustees will have the documents to facilitate that. A good trustee will have experience in settling estates upon the death of the trust holder.

What Rights Does the Trustee Have?

The trustee does not have any rights to your assets or the right to make decisions about your assets without your approval.

Section 6.07: Foreclosure

A foreclosure takes place when the homeowner's loan is secured using the property deed as collateral and the owner fails to make the loan payments to the lender. Contrary to popular belief a foreclosure is a lengthy process in which the homeowner is given ample time to remedy the situation. The process varies from state to state, but in many states, the homeowner is given up to four months to avoid foreclosure.

In the early stages of foreclosure, the borrower is given written notice that he or she has defaulted or failed to make regular loan payments. A declaration of default is prepared by the lender and submitted to the recorder's office. Next, the lender notifies the buyer that the property will be sold. Twenty days to one month later, the lender may begin advertising the foreclosure sale. At this point, a sale notice is posted on the property. The borrower then has three months to catch up on the debt. If the borrower fails to remedy the default within three months, the property can be sold at an auction. The trustee and the lender set the minimum bid. The sale is final. However, some states allow the borrower some time after the sale to remedy the default and revoke the sale. When the trustee and the note holder are not the same entity, the trustee is paid first and the note holder is paid the remaining balance from the sale. Readers should refer to the state-by-state review as foreclosure procedures vary from state to state. Those wishing to purchase at a foreclosure auction must be prepared to produce cash or its equivalent. These sales do not provide for a financing opportunity.

Case Study: Eric Bozinny

Properties can be purchased in many non-traditional ways. As the following story explains, foreclosure auctions are one alternative to buyers. However, these actions are handled differently in each state. A buyer should get more information from a reputable broker or real estate attorney before attempting to buy in this way.

My wife and I went 25 miles north into Snohomish County, just north of Seattle, with a few properties targeted at the trustees' sale there. Foreclosures are handled differently when the loan is secured by a deed of trust versus a mortgage. In Washington, the vast majority of loans are secured by deeds of trust. In other states, mortgages are the norm. The biggest difference? The foreclosure process. Mortgage foreclosure auctions are managed by the court, with the sheriff's department often handling them. Furthermore, in some states, the original owner actually has a statutory period of time during which he can gain back title to the

Case Study: Eric Bozinny

property if the debt is brought current or paid off. This is clearly a disadvantage to the buyers at auctions. An advantage of a trustee auctions is that cash payment of the property is not due until some time after the sale date. In trustee auctions, the title is effectively wiped clean with a foreclosure sale, and the buyer owns it outright. However, cash, typically a cashier's check, is needed at the time of sale.

Real Estate Owned

Real estate owned (REO) is property foreclosed on, but still owned by a lender. There could be many reasons for this, but the primary one is the auction did not yield a minimum bid and the property did not sell. REO properties will sit on the lender's books until someone comes along and makes an offer. Sometimes lenders will make very favorable loans and even eat closing costs to get rid of these liabilities. Typically, mortgages made on these properties, with in some cases 100 percent financing, are kept in house, meaning the buyer will not be forced to meet secondary market terms. Also, know that real estate agents can make huge profits from these deals and most will be happy to help you find REOs.

Section 6.08: Creative Financing

Seller Financed

A seller who is looking to get out of a property quickly or wants to spread the income tax bill created by the sale over several years and owns the property outright is the perfect candidate for seller financed buying. This means the seller holds a deed of trust just as any other lender would while the buyer makes monthly payments to the seller for the entire value of the real estate. When the property has been paid off, the seller gives the deed to the buyer who then owns the property without a lien. With this alternative, the seller may even let you move in without a down payment.

Apartment buildings make great candidates as after a number of years owners can become exhausted by the constant management demands and look to unload the property without a huge year-end tax bill. If you do not want to be a proprietor either, consider the tenants-in-common option. Refer to the tenants-in-common section later in this chapter.

Buy a Smaller House Now and Add On Later, Part I

If you are unable to get financing to meet your square footage needs, seriously consider buying a smaller house and hunkering down for one or two years while it gains equity. Later, you can refinance, pulling out that equity to add on additional space. This is great advice for young couples planning a family, but not until later. Most people can expect income increases as they pursue their careers, making this option that much easier. This is an excellent strategy for those trying to buy into high markets like Tucson, where I live. Remodeling can give you a tax break also, but check tax codes as they change from year to year. Of course, economic factors will affect this strategy. For example, the cost of building supplies tripled just a few months after the 2006 Hurricane Katrina disaster. You will want to consider what is happening around you just as you would when making any major decision.

Here is the down side to this plan. Some types of remodeling add more value than others. The cost of adding a garage can typically be recouped at resale. Other types of additions will only add 50 percent to 75 percent of their cost to the resale value of your house. However, if you are in an expensive market like Los Angeles, you may not have any other realistic way to secure more square footage. Here are a few points to keep in mind.

- Depleting more than 20 percent of the property's equity could leave you high and dry should you need that resource later in an emergency.

- Expect the contractor's bill to be 10 percent to 20 percent more than the estimate.

- You will be borrowing against your home. If you cannot repay the borrowed funds, you will lose your home.

You have several financing options. Cash out financing allows the homeowner to replace their existing mortgage with a larger one for cash. The cash can be used in any way the homeowner wishes. If interest rates have gone down since you bought the property, this is an excellent option. A home equity loan will provide the homeowner with a predetermined amount of money, which is given in a lump sum. It is repaid with interest that will typically be higher than the original mortgage. A home equity line of credit works like a credit card. Homeowners can withdraw up to a predetermined maximum amount. The money is withdrawn in the form of a check written out to you by you with the property serving as collateral.

Buy a Smaller House Now and Add On Later, Part II

Other options are available to those not wishing to borrow against their homes or not having sufficient equity to get the needed funds. Here are some alternatives.

Title 1 loans are available to lower income people. These loans, guaranteed by the Federal Housing Administration, can be given in amounts as high as $25,000. They are obtained through traditional lenders and are tax deductible. They will only be given for a good reason. For example, a family could use one of these loans to add on if they were expecting a baby or had to undertake the care of a relative. They cannot be used for luxury or elective remodeling.

Construction loans provide an alternative when the property does not have enough equity to borrow sufficient funds as a home equity loan or line of credit. However, because these loans depend less on collateral, borrowers must have excellent credit and show ample ability to repay to secure a construction loan. With a construction loan, the borrower will pay interest only during construction. After the renovation, the home will have more value. At this point an entirely new mortgage that includes the construction bill will be started. It will use the home with its new value as collateral.

The homeowner can borrow money from himself or herself through a 401(k) loan. This is an excellent way to borrow because you pay interest, but you pay it to yourself. The problem with this type of loan is if you lose your job before the loan is repaid, the entire sum will be due immediately. Otherwise, the borrower will be forced to pay heavy taxes and early withdrawal penalties.

A personal loan is safe because it does not use your home as collateral, but it is difficult to obtain for individuals without exceptional credit. With a personal loan, you get the loan because the lender believes you will repay it. However, the lack of collateral makes it risky. Consequently, lenders charge high interest rates on these types of loans. Typically, borrowers are charged double-digit interest.

Ways of Financing Closing Costs and a Down Payment

A Second Mortgage

Buyers can sometimes pay closing costs through a second mortgage. The money can be borrowed from the lender, if they will allow it, or from the seller. Offering the seller more interest than he or she could make investing elsewhere certainly works. Considering the seller will receive a substantial sum of cash when the property sells, your offer stands a good chance of being accepted. A great feature is both parties can work out repayment terms that best suit them.

Offer a Higher Price to the Seller in Exchange for Closing Fees

Buyers not wishing to deplete their savings can ask the seller to roll closing costs into the sale price. This is very simple. You just raise the final price by the amount you will owe at closing and the seller assumes the payment of all fees at the closing. The seller will not need to produce a large amount of cash up front because the fees will be paid by the escrow agent out of the sale proceeds before they are given to the seller.

Add the Closing Fees to the Mortgage

In the past, this was an unacceptable lending practice. In modern times, more lenders are willing to do it. Buyers simply ask their lenders to roll closing costs into the mortgage. Of course, this will only work if the property's appraised value is high enough to cover the extra expense without pushing the loan past 80 percent of the property's value. Otherwise, borrowers will be faced with buying mortgage insurance, which will cost more in the end than closing costs. Be warned that some lenders will only agree to do this in exchange for a higher interest rate. The added interest may cost more over time than closing costs.

Performance Bond

A performance bond is a legal promise between two people for work in exchange for something else. The something else could be money or it could be land, closing costs, or a down payment. If the seller needs something, you may be able to trade your services for closing costs of part of the down payment.

Trading

Another term for trading is bartering. If you have something of interest to the seller such as a boat, a vacation time-share, or jewelry, offer to trade it for closing costs. Bartering is a beneficial and under-used means of payment.

Bifurcate

This legal term just means more than one money transfer is involved with the title transfer. To bifurcate a property means the seller agrees to borrow part of what you owe as a secondary mortgage. In some cases, this will allow you to avoid mortgage insurance and a down payment, making the deal. Unlike a wraparound loan, bifurcation allows the seller to have all of his or her money up front. However, this scenario means the seller must take a risk that you will not pay back what has been borrowed on your behalf. Of course, the seller will become a creditor to the buyer, meaning the seller can foreclose should the buyer fail to pay the secondary mortgage.

Unfortunately, bifurcation caused the savings and loan crash in the 1980s when many people built real estate portfolios based on paper only without any real money to back up anything. This became a very real problem when housing prices fell and property flippers discovered they could not count on making a profit to pay back their debts. Unable to manage these debts, their properties went into foreclosure. However, the housing market had fallen, meaning the savings and loans could not get back what had been lent out. Today, many lenders will not finance if the property has a pre-existing secondary mortgage. To protect themselves they force the buyers to sign an affidavit stating no secondary financing is involved in the closing. To get around this you must do a two-step closing. First, the purchase money mortgage is taken out and the property goes to closing. After closing, a secondary mortgage is created to cover the down payment. However, the buyer and seller must ensure that neither loan is callable, meaning the lender can demand a complete repayment at any time. If the lender were to discover a secondary mortgage had been established immediately after closing, although not in violation of the signed affidavit, the lender could get cold feet and recall the purchase loan.

Charging Closing Costs to a Credit Card

Although taking a cash advance from a credit card will be interest expensive, it may be a good option if you can repay it quickly. A high interest rate in the short term will cost less than a lower interest rate paid over 30 years.

Reduced Interest Owner-Occupied Mortgages

Many lenders will offer a reduced interest rate if the owner intends to occupy the property as a primary residence. The reason is that an owner will be more likely to pay a mortgage if the payment is required to keep a roof over his head, so that the loan presents less risk to the lender. Knowing this, buyers should always intend to move into their purchase if this option is possible. To get the lower interest rate you must only intend to stay at the residence for an indefinite period. What you do later is up to you. No laws regulating how long you stay exist.

First-Time Home Buyer Loan

Many lenders will give first-time home buyers low interest rates and allow them to make smaller down payments. Make sure your lender knows you are a first time home buyer. You do not necessarily have to be making your first purchase to qualify. If you have not owned a home in the past three years, that may be long enough to qualify.

A Home Equity Loan as Part of the Initial Financing

Besides closing costs, a home equity loan can be used for the financing of the principal. This is typically done as an 80/20 percent split. This financing set-up can help you to avoid mortgage insurance while allowing you to borrow more than 80 percent of the appraised value of the property.

A No-Qualifying Loan

Sometimes qualifying for a mortgage is not necessary, the case if you are borrowing less than 80 percent of the value of the property by making a large down payment. Your large down payment reduces the loan's risk because you have much to lose should you default. If the down payment is large enough, the lender may not even run a credit check. However, if you lie and later the lender has a reason to verify your stated income, which will happen if you default, you will be faced with fraud charges. This type of loan is more common in a slow market when lenders are trying to push loans.

A Low Doc Loan

This type of loan only requires a credit report and the verification of an available down payment. For this reason, it is the perfect solution for self-employed buyers who frequently have difficulty proving their income, especially when a substantial portion of it was paid in cash. When applying for conventional loans, self-employed persons will need to show two years of tax records plus many additional years of profit. This leaves a person who has been self-employed for less than two years out in the cold. As is the case with a no-qualifying loan, if the lender checks your income later and verifies that it was falsely represented, you will be faced with fraud charges.

Interest Only Mortgage

An interest only mortgage is just that. The borrower will pay only interest during the life of the loan and make a balloon payment of the principal at the end. Obviously, this type of financing is not for everyone. However, if you are paid on commission in which some months are lucrative and others are not, you are a good candidate. Someone who receives a large yearly profit share payment, which represents a substantial part of his or her income, is also a good candidate. Other excellent candidates are:

- Buyers who expect to have a lump-sum payment in the future from a source such as a trust.

- Business owner with unpredictable monthly income but a certain overall yearly income.

- A buyer who intends to invest securely what would be paid toward the principal.

- Someone intending to flip the property.

- Someone who only intends to own the property for a year or two.

Generally, lenders do not recommend this type of financing for the average person. You will need to have a specific motivating reason. You should not consider this if you do not have a plan in place to provide for the balloon payment.

Those considering this option must understand that this type of borrowing does not create a savings for the borrower. In fact, it creates the opposite. Interest-only loans can be useful tools for individuals in some situations, but they are not right for the average person. Let me give an example. If a borrower pays only $500 for the first five years of a 30-year $100,000 loan at 6 percent interest, the supposed savings will be $99.56 each month. However, the borrower must face either a balloon payment at the end or change over to an amortizing loan. An amortizing loan with the same rates will cost $644.31 a month. As you can see, the borrower is now losing any savings originally gained at the rate of $44.75 per month. If the borrower pays off the loan over the next 25 years, the savings created will be lost over the next 11 years. Clearly, interest-only loans benefit only those who have a solid financial reason like those listed above and can make a balloon payment at the end.

Shared Ownership

If you simply cannot afford to own a property on your own, consider shared ownership. There are several ways to hold a community title. Refer to Chapter 4, section 4.04. Parents and other relatives may be willing to invest with you. You can buy them out later, possibly profiting them, but you must work that out.

Condominiums, townhouses, and duplexes offer other cheaper home ownership alternatives. These properties will gain equity over time just like a single-family house. Take advantage of this. Start out in a shared dwelling. Sell it later, cashing out the equity, which will increase your down payment for a single-family house.

Tenants-in-Common

In areas like Los Angeles where housing is expensive, people share buildings as tenants-in-common. Doing this is equivalent to apartment living, but each tenant is the owner of a percentage of the building with all of the tenants' ownership adding up to 100 percent. On the down side, tenants-in-common are legally complex as far as financing and organizing repairs.

Joint Tenancy

Joint tenancy is another option in expensive real estate areas. Joint tenancy is equivalent to having a roommate, but each party is a 50 percent owner, not a renter. However, one tenant can transfer ownership rights without the permission of the other tenant. If your joint tenant decides to sell his or her half, a buyer can be chosen without your consent. This means that if the house has not been split, you will have a new roommate you did not choose.

Co-housing

Co-housing is much like tenants-in-common except the tenants live in a communally owned neighborhood instead of a building. This type of ownership can spell a savings of as much as 20 percent, putting single-family housing within the reach of more people. Savings is created because the cost of the land is shared. For example, imagine I could purchase five acres of land for $5,000. If I purchase the same five acres of land with 10 other people, I would only pay $500. However, I would have access to the entire 10 acres. Moreover, additional pooled resources could allow for building facilities I could never afford on my own like a swimming pool or gym. All the while, I am able to enjoy the privacy of my own house.

Lease Purchase

Lease to own can be an excellent option if you have less than perfect credit. It is a standard lease with the option to purchase at a predetermined time. This situation has good and bad points. Many of these contracts will put part of the monthly payment into a "purchase fund" and the rest into the owner's pocket. If you decide to purchase, part of your previous monthly payments are subtracted from the sale price. However, as I said, part of the payment went into the owner's pocket, meaning that if you stay in the lease-to-own for a long enough period, the property will cost more than if you had purchased it outright. This option will not create a complete escape from the rent racket, but it is an alternative option for those with poor credit.

Susu Saver

Susu saving is a way of saving as part of a community. Each participant contributes a fixed amount at a fixed interval, for example, $30 every week. At predetermined times each member in turn gets to cash out the pool. The amounts are usually under $5,000, but if used in combination with other previously given suggestions, the pot could be used to fund closing costs. If you participate in several susus, you could fund both closing costs and a down payment. These funds are based on the honor system.

Less Than Perfect Credit

B/C Loans

As you may have guessed, B/C stands for bad credit. In an effort not to offend, many lenders will simply refer to these as B/C loans. Lower income borrowers who cannot meet the credit criteria of a conforming loan through Fannie Mae and Freddie Mac, may be able to get a non-secured loan with a higher interest rate. Potential applicants include those who have completed a bankruptcy, previously foreclosed, or have a history of late payments.

In exchange for a higher interest rate, some lenders will offer 100 percent financing with no money down. Understandably, no money down in addition to less than perfect credit adds up to a great deal of risk. Therefore, borrowers with poor credit should do everything within their power to create as little additional risk to the lender as possible to hold down their interest rate.

Debt Consolidation

Debt consolidation is an excellent way for people to get back on track with their credit especially when many small debts formed an overwhelming amount. While this preliminary step causes a buyer to need to delay a home purchase, obtaining a conforming mortgage and a lower interest rate will make the wait worthwhile.

Ways to Improve Your Credit

If your credit is a little bruised, there are some ways to improve it quickly. First, if you have missed some payments to a credit card or other debt, get current as quickly as possible. Many people mistakenly think once they get behind, the credit damage has been done. Therefore, they might as well take their time getting caught up. This is not true. Delinquent payments will cause your credit score to drop further over time. The more time that passes the further your score will drop. Creditors report late payments to the three major credit bureaus every 30 to 60 days. On the upside, your tardiness will not be reported if it is fewer than 29 days.

Always pay more than the minimum balance on your credit cards even if it is only slightly more. Many consumers are not aware of this, but minimum credit card payments will lower your credit score because they create the impression that you are struggling to pay off the debt. The more months each year that you pay the minimum balance the lower your credit score will be. Additionally, you probably will not be able to pay off the card unless you pay more than the minimum balance due to the high interest rates charged by credit card companies. Therefore, begin paying more than the minimum balance immediately.

Avoid creating more revolving credit and eliminate revolving credit. Store credit cards predominantly create revolving credit. Even if these cards have zero balances, keeping too many of them will lower your credit score. One factor of your credit score is your debt to income ratio. Multiple credit cards, even with zero balances, will increase your debt to income ratio because they create the possibility of future debt. Therefore, closing out your store credit cards and only maintaining one or two major credit cards with moderate lines of credit will make your score go up immediately.

Consumers should avoid credit repair services. This may sound surprising, but your application to a credit repair service will be reported to the three major credit bureaus and lower you score by 100 points immediately. These services should only be sought by those who are really in trouble and not by those who just need a little help. The average American has a credit score of only 600. Know that a bankruptcy will lower a credit score to 500 immediately. Consider this: if your score is already at 600 and a credit repair service application causes it to drop by 100 points to 500, you will have bankruptcy level credit without the clean slate benefits of a bankruptcy. Consolidating your debt, paying more than the minimum monthly payment on your credit cards, paying on time, and avoiding revolving credit are the best ways to make your score go up quickly.

Rural Housing Service Programs (RHS)

Private Citizen Programs

This government agency, which is part of the Department of Agriculture, works to assist lower income rural Americans purchase real estate and make home renovations and repairs. It also makes financing available to elderly or disabled rural residents of multi-unit housing buildings to ensure they are able to make rent payments.

The Direct Loan Program

The RHS has multiple programs. The direct loan program, frequently referred to as section 502, provides single individuals and families with home loans at low affordable interest rates. The loan funds come directly from the Housing and Community Facilities Program and are guaranteed by the RHS. Because these loans are non-conforming, they can be given to individuals who would not qualify for Fannie Mae or Freddie Mac loans. Most of these loans are made to families with median incomes below 80 percent of the other people living in their community. However, this 80 percent marker is not a rule and those with higher incomes may qualify. The loan funds can be used to purchase a new home or to renovate and/or repair an existing home.

The Loan Guarantee Program

The loan guarantee program or section 502 of the Housing and Community Facilities Program (HCFP) guarantees loans made by private sector lenders. The buyer borrows from and repays a lender directly, allowing the program to help more people than it would if working alone with its own funds. To guarantee a loan means that if the borrower defaults, the HCFP would pay the loan.

> **TIP**
>
> The section 502 program allows families and individuals to borrow 100 percent of the appraised value of their home without mortgage insurance eliminating the need for a down payment, frequently a barrier to lower income people, opening up home ownership to more people.

The Mutual Self-Help Program

The mutual self-help program or section 523 of the Housing and Community Facilities Program allows future homeowners to make a sweat investment instead of a monetary investment in their home purchase. Those wanting to build a home must do at least 65 percent of the work themselves, but because the HCFP will give credit for the work, it allows them to pay less for it. Applicants work in groups of five to twelve people, each working on the homes of all the others as well as their own. All of the team members are permitted to move into their own home when every other team member's home has been completed. Typically, section 523 is used in conjunction with section 502.

In addition to helping homeowners, technical assistance grants and loans are given to nonprofit and local government organizations, who supervise groups of five to twelve enrollees in the Self-Help Program.

The Rural Housing Site Loan

The rural housing site loan or section 523 was established to work in conjunction with section 524, explained above. It provides financing for the purchase and development of a building site in a rural area to those with low and middle incomes. However, non-profit organizations, federally recognized tribes and public bodies are also eligible to receive this funding.

The Home Repair Loan and Grant Program

Section 504 or the home repair loan and grant program assists families whose homes need repairs or renovations. It will also grant money for renovations to accommodate a disabled person. For example, money can be granted or loaned to perform major plumbing repairs, add a handicapped accessible bathroom, construct a ramp system for a disabled person, or install insulation. Special consideration is given to home improvement applicants that are 65 or older. When money is loaned and not granted, it is loaned at 1 percent interest.

Rural Rental Housing Direct Loan and Guaranteed Loan Programs

These programs, sections 538 and 515, are like the direct loan and loan guarantee programs but for constructing a multiple family dwelling for low-income families. Those occupying the property must be or low or moderate income and be elderly, handicapped, or disabled persons with incomes that do not exceed 115 percent of the median income of those living in the surrounding area. The program will guarantee up to 90 percent of the loan funds received from a private lender.

Housing Preservation Grant Program

This grant, section 533, is available to non-profit organizations, local governments, and federally recognized tribes to renovate existing multiple family residences as a whole. Funds are given to and used by individual residents of multiple family dwellings for the renovation or repair of their unit or private home. The funds can be used in coordination with additional resources from private donations or the local government.

Business Programs

Non-Profit Facilities and the U.S. Department of Agriculture (USDA) Rural

Business Service Business and Industry Direct and Guaranteed Loans and Grants

Many of the programs available to private citizens such as the loan guarantee program and the direct loan program are also available to non-profit organizations, assisting them with building repairs as well as upstart costs. People wanting to start rural businesses that will create jobs are eligible to receive the USDA rural business service business and industry guaranteed loans and grants. The USDA offers a variety of programs under the business and industry loan and grant heading. The following is a brief explanation.

- *Business and Industry Guaranteed Loans*
  These loans can be used to create industry that creates jobs to stimulate the local rural economy. Successful applicants must receive loan funds through federally or state chartered and approved banks, credit unions, or savings and loans. The loan money can be used for any purpose except agriculture. The business must be outside the boundaries of a city or town with fewer than 50,000 residents.

- *Intermediary Relending Loans*
  These loans are made to public bodies to relend to a rural community for the establishment of businesses, expansion of businesses, and community development. The final loan recipient must be in or outside a town with fewer than 25,000.

- *Rural Business Enterprise Grants*
  These grants are initially given to non-profit corporations and local governments. However, the money must be used to help young businesses to expand and thrive in rural communities of fewer than 50,000. Individual small businesses themselves are not eligible to apply but must work in conjunction with the assisting organization. However, the grant money can be

used to purchase land, buildings, establish parking facilities, gain street access, and facilitate small business development in general.

- *Rural Economic Development Loans*
  These loans are initially given to electric and utility providers and are re-lent to small rural businesses to help them establish services and create jobs. The re-lent money must be given with 0 percent to 1 percent interest and can be lent for up to 10 years.

- *Rural Economic Development Grants*
  These grants are initially given to electric and utility providers, but like their counterpart, the rural economic development loan, they must be distributed to rural small businesses to help them establish services and create jobs.

The above listed programs are just those that directly relate to real estate. Other rural business assistance programs exist. Interested parties should go to **http://www.rurdev.usda.gov/il/whoweare. htm**, to find the nearest rural development office.

Funding for Community Programs

Community Programs is a department of the USDA and is designed to assist with the development of community facilities in rural areas. In reality there are three programs encompassed by the community programs department. They are the community facilities direct loan program, the community facilities guaranteed loan program, and the community facilities grant program. These facilities can include but are not limited to public libraries, schools, child care facilities, clinics, fire and police stations, and community centers. The community programs give assistance to communities whose populations are under 20,000. The money must be borrowed or granted to and by a public entity such as a municipality, county, tribal council, or school district. This body must have the legal authority to borrow, repay, and maintain the public facility on behalf of its constituents. The repayment loan terms are based on tax assessments, pre-existing debt, and the expected operational costs of the facility, with three interest rate levels available. Typically, a study must be done of the expected benefits of the facility, and public bonds are created to facilitate repayment. The money can be borrowed directly from the program or borrowed from a private lender and guaranteed up to 90 percent by the community program.

Housing Application Packaging Grants

This grant funds non-profit organizations and tax-exempt public agencies who help the public apply for the other previously mentioned programs. The funds may be used to facilitate prescreening for eligibility, ensure the completion and accuracy of applications, and help applicants understand the various options offered by each program. The grant money may also be used to train employees who will assist the applicants.

 Readers can get more information about these government programs at http://www.rurdev.usda.gov/rhs/index.html.

Sale Leaseback

Leaseback presents a way for buyers to break into mature markets. A lack of cash flow is the reason businesses in the United States fail 70 percent of the time. Sale leaseback is a way businesses can liquidate real estate without losing access to needed production facilities and warehousing. The process is very simple. A seller deeds a property to a buyer for cash, and the buyer simultaneously leases the property back to the seller. Typically, the seller can secure a lease of 15 to 20 years with optional renewals. However, these deals are made with simple fee ownership created through the transference of a warranty deed, which means the titleholder, the buyer, will have the right to own the property throughout his or her lifetime or the lifetime of the purchasing business and can will it upon death. In other words, simple fee ownership is forever.

This type of transaction can greatly benefit both the buyer and seller. The seller can raise capital without creating a debt lien while maintaining access to the real estate. The buyer gets a tenant-occupied business rental site that will make money from day one. The buyer can count on a predictable, consistent return on the investment through rents paid by the seller. Because the seller has been managing the property, this type of real estate investment requires minimal hands-on management. Last, this new investment will begin a new depreciation tax allowance schedule, freeing pre-existing profits from taxes. If the property was financed, the interest can be deducted from the investor's taxes.

In terms of the seller, sale leaseback can provide an exit strategy for a business owner looking toward retirement, or it can facilitate the expansion of a business, involving moving to another facility. The 1031 exchange option of our current tax code allows capital gains tax to be avoided by exchanging the equity of one investment for another. Business owners must seek professional tax consultation before initiating this type of transaction. Often the cash raised from the sale-leaseback is greater than the book value of the property sold. Once again, contact a professional real estate agent before undertaking this transaction.

Hard Money and Bridge Loans

Hard money and bridge loans are real estate loans that use the property itself as collateral. However, the collateral's value is based on the quick sale price of the property. A quick sale is a sale that occurs in one to four months. This is sometimes called the loan-to-value and is typically 60 percent to 70 percent of the property's real value. The term real value means today's purchase price. Most lenders will only fund as the primary creditor, meaning if the borrower defaults, they are paid first. If the lender does allow another party to be the primary creditor, we call it a mezzanine loan instead of a hard money loan.

Hard money and bridge loans tend to be fast and are typically arranged because a business has a last-minute problem such as unforeseen costs. For this reason, these loans have a bad reputation even though this is a legitimate financing structure. Hard money loans are typically issued at a high interest rates and are almost never issued by a commercial bank. Borrowers must go directly to a hard moneylender.

The primary difference between a bridge loan and a hard money loan is that a bridge loan is used for commercial or investment property that will not qualify for a conforming loan. The reasons vary, but typically, the property is in transition, perhaps because of a death or foreclosure. Hard money loans are asset-based loans that can signify financial distress as they are commonly used to carry the owner through some financial difficulty.

A typical hard money or bridge loan for a real estate purchase will be structured with 60 percent loan funds, 20 percent equity from the borrower and 15 percent from a secondary loan.

Blanket Loans

When a hard money loan is formed, the original mortgage lender must be paid off. This allows the hard moneylender to become the primary creditor. If the loan to value, discussed previously, will not facilitate this, the lender must establish a cross lien instead. This cross lien loan is sometimes referred to as a blanket loan and is mostly used by commercial real estate investors.

Case Study: Eric Bozinny

As mentioned in the previous case study, properties can be purchased in many non-traditional ways. Using your monthly income to build equity is always a better option than paying rent. While discussing this book with my husband, he made these comments.

We purchased our single-family house after several years of just considering home ownership. Honestly, it was never a serious consideration. I thought getting into real estate would be hard or something that wealthy people did. I did not understand the different ways real estate can be financed and all of the programs available to help people buy. If I had known how easy it would be, I would have purchased years before. When I think of all the years I spent paying rent when I could have been investing that money into my own future, I feel sick. My advice to everyone is to jump in. Do not wait for the market to be perfect. The market will never be quite right in some way. An experienced real estate professional can help you work any market situation to your advantage. Start asking questions. Discover how to purchase in a way that suits you and your life, but definitely stop paying rent.

chapter seven

Real Estate Settlement Procedures Act (RESPA)

Section 7.01: What is RESPA? What was RESPA Established to Prohibit?

The Real Estate Settlement Procedures Act (RESPA) was passed in 1974 to help consumers shop for settlement services and to eliminate kickbacks that can increase the costs of those services. While protecting consumers from unscrupulous real estate service providers, it works to help them understand the costs associated with closing by requiring that disclosures regarding transaction fees be made. Before RESPA was enacted, some companies that provide real estate sales, mortgage, and settlement were giving business referral kickbacks to each other at the expense of consumers. Additionally, they were advertising services at one highly competitive price, but adding on questionable transaction fees at the time of closing.

Section 7.02: RESPA Requirements for Lenders

The first disclosure must be made with the loan application. At this time the lender must provide a universal booklet, available to all lenders, that gives information about real estate settlement services. The borrower must be provided with a good faith estimate of the charges the borrower will pay at closing. If the borrower is required to use a certain settlement provider, that must be disclosed with the good faith estimate. The lender must tell the borrower if they intend to service the loan or if it will be serviced by another lender. Last, the borrower must be informed who will handle complaints. If the lender does not provide this information at the time of the loan application, it must be provided within three business days. This may happen, for example, if the loan is obtained online. If the loan is turned down, the lender will not be responsible for providing this information.

Section 7.03: RESPA Protections for Borrowers

RESPA protects borrowers from fees associated with kickbacks. It protects consumers by prohibiting any party from giving or accepting anything of value as payment for a referral in conjunction with a mortgage loan. All parties are banned from giving or receiving anything of value for services not provided.

Some critics aver that the public still faces kickbacks and unclear service fees in spite of the act. For example, lenders select their own title insurance agents who charge fees that must be paid by borrowers, and borrowers often use service providers recommended to them by their lenders because they are unfamiliar with their local real estate market and do not know where to go for these services.

Section 7.04: RESPA Covered Loans

Mortgage loans secured with a deed of trust for one to four family residential properties are covered by RESPA. This includes initial purchase loans, HUD, FHA and VA loans, assumptions, refinances, home improvement loans, and home equity lines of credit. Refinancing does fall under the realm of RESPA. However, simple extension agreements are not considered to be refinancing subject to RESPA if the existing obligation is not satisfied and replaced with a new one.

Section 7.05: What Types of Loans are Exempt?

Based on 24 CFR 3500.5(b)(3) of the RESPA law, bridge loans are exempt from RESPA. A construction loan is exempt unless the same lender is doing the permanent financing, or the loan is financing the transfer of the title to the primary owner, or the loan term is for two years or more.

Business purpose loans are exempt. Exemption is determined by Regulation Z and involves an examination of the loan size and the purpose of the loan. However, a lender can make the exemption determination at the time of prequalification.

Rental properties fall into the business category and are exempt. However, certain criteria should be considered before exemption is assumed. First, the property is only a business property if the owner does not plan to live on the premises for more than 14 days every year. However, if the property contains more than three units other than the one to be occupied by the owner, it moves back into the business property category. If the loan is for the purpose of improving the owner-occupied rental property, it is considered a business loan.

Loans for the purchase of more than 25 acres are exempt. Despite the fact that the acreage may be for residential use, it is considered to be business exempt for farming. Temporary financing is exempt. Temporary financing is not defined by the law but is assumed to be construction loans, bridge loans, and swing loans. The reader should note that if permanent financing will be obtained later from the same lender, RESPA will apply to the temporary financing. Mortgage loans secured by vacant land are exempt unless a residential building will be put on the structure within two years of the land purchase. Assumptions are also exempt from RESPA, although if lender approval is required to complete the transaction, RESPA will apply.

Loan conversions are also exempt from RESPA. The exemption will apply only to conversions to different loan terms that are consistent with provisions of original mortgage. For the exemption to apply, the conversion cannot result in a new note.

A loan transferred into the secondary market is not covered by RESPA. More important, RESPA does not dictate what must be disclosed to the borrower. In this case, referral fees and kickbacks are not prohibited. However, mortgage broker transactions that are not table-funded are not considered secondary market transactions. Table-funding means a loan is funded by an advance of loan funds, and the loan is assigned to the person advancing the funds.

Section 7.06: RESPA, Civil Lawsuits, and Filing Complaints

RESPA does not clearly define penalties for lenders who do not give the required information to borrowers. This task is left up to bank regulators. Individual borrowers are given varying periods to initiate a lawsuit for RESPA violations. If a suit settlement is awarded the borrower, they may be granted actual damages as well as punitive damages when a pattern of noncompliance is established. The statute of limitations is determined by the section of the law violated. Consumers can go to **http://www.hud.gov/offices** for more information.

Consumers with loan servicing complaints must contact their lenders in writing and explain the complaint in detail. Borrowers should also send a copy of the complaint to:

> Director, Office of RESPA and Interstate Land Sales
> US Department of Housing and Urban Development
> Room 9154, 451 7th Street SW, Washington, DC 20410

The lender is given 60 days to respond. The loan servicer, if different from the lender, must respond within 20 days. The loan servicer must act to resolve the complaint or provide an explanation of their position within 60 days. However, borrowers must continue to make loan payments when moving through the complaint process.

Violators of RESPA's section 8, which prohibits kickbacks, referral fees, and charging fees for services not performed can be prosecuted under federal law and face a $10,000 fine and/or one year of imprisonment. The violator may also be sued in civil court for the loss plus three times the loss.

Section 7.07: RESPA Requirements for Sellers

In accordance with RESPA's section 9, home sellers are banned from requiring home buyers to purchase title insurance from a particular insurance provider as a condition of the sale. Those violating section 9 can be forced by a court of law to reimburse the seller for the title insurance plus three times the cost.

Section 7.08: RESPA Closing Requirements

At closing the settlement statement must show all charges to both buyer and seller in connection with the transaction. RESPA dictates that the buyer be permitted to see the settlement statement at least one day before the predetermined closing date. The settlement statement must contain all of the amounts due and owed as of the day the document is presented to the buyer. These fees include the actual costs of the loan transaction. The closing agent may present separate settlement forms to the buyer and seller if the parties choose to conduct closing separately. If either party chooses not to attend settlement in person, the settlement statement must be delivered as soon as is practically possible after settlement.

In accordance with RESPA, the buyer will be given the initial escrow statement at closing, itemizing estimated taxes, insurance premiums, and any other charges to be paid from the mortgage escrow account. Traditionally, this statement is given at closing, but legally the closing agent has 45 days to deliver it to the buyer.

Each year the loan servicer must give the borrower an escrow statement to comply with RESPA which summarizes all escrow account deposits and withdrawals as well as payments due for service to the servicer. It will notify the borrower of any surpluses or shortages in the escrow account and how those discrepancies need to be resolved.

Finally, RESPA requires a servicing transfer statement be given to the borrower if the servicer sells or assigns the servicing responsibilities to another party. The information must be provided 15 days before the loan is transferred and must include name, address, a toll free phone number, and date of the transfer.

Section 7.09: AfBA

The AfBA (Affiliated Business Arrangement Disclosure) was established by a 1992 amendment to RESPA. A lender may give a referral to a borrower if the borrower is given an Affiliated Business Arrangement Disclosure (AfBA) prior to the referral. The AfBA must describe the affiliation and business arrangement that exists between the two parties. An exception is made if the lender refers the borrower to an attorney, credit reporting agency, or real estate appraiser who represents the lender with the understanding that the borrower is not required to accept services from these parties. The law assumes the lender has the right to be represented to the borrower by these parties.

The 1992 RESPA amendment also allowed for real estate agents to affiliate with other service providers such as mortgage brokers and discount their services for the use of these service provider. However, the affiliation between these service providers must be disclosed in writing to the consumer before she or he is referred to another company.

In 1996 HUD issued a RESPA new and final RESPA rule that a company may not compensate its employees for referring customers to another company.

Section 7.10: The AfBA Safe Harbor Test

Certain guidelines must be followed to prevent an AfBA from being a violation of RESPA's Section 8. First, a written disclosure of the relationship between the lender and the service provider being referred must be given to the borrower. Second the borrower must not be required as a condition of the loan to use the referred service provider. The fees to be charged to the borrower by the lender must not be affected by the decision not to use or to use the assistance of the referred party. Finally, nothing of value may be exchanged between the lender and the referred service provider in exchange for the referral. Any payments made between the parties disclosed in the AfBA must be for services rendered and not for the referral.

Additional Department of Housing and Urban Development (HUD) Criteria for AfBAs

Out of concern that abuses are still possible in spite of RESPA's Section 8 and the AfBA exception policy, HUD established their own criteria, involving an independent examination of the capitalization, employees, management, location, services provided, subcontracting, marketing, and referrals in the event the referral arrangement is deemed questionable.

Section 7.11: RESPA and Escrow Accounts

RESPA limits the amount a lender can require a borrower to put into escrow. It does this by limiting the input by its purpose. The required money must be used for property taxes, insurance, or other charges related to the property. Although RESPA does not ever require an escrow account, some other governmental lenders do. To protect the borrower, the lender may not require more than 1/12 of the total yearly disbursements be put into the escrow account. If the account has a shortage, that may also be required of the borrower. To prevent shortages, the lender may require a cushion payment of no more than 1/6 of the total yearly disbursements to be taken from the account.

Section 7.12: RESPA and Thank You Gifts

Many of us, being polite people, like to send thank you cards and perhaps a small gift, such as a bottle of wine or food basket when we have been treated well. Unfortunately, these small tokens of appreciation are violations of RESPA. The law clearly states that nothing of value may be exchanged. No matter how innocent we may perceive a small gift to be, the law is clear. I strongly recommend simply making a thank you phone call and leaving things at that.

chapter eight

A State by State Review

Section 8.01: ALABAMA

Land titles are checked how far back into the past?

Land titles are researched back 40 to 60 years. Of course, if the title insurer had a valid reason, the title would be researched further. One should note that this rule is a custom and not a state law. If a search is impossible, for example, because of the destruction of records, the seller can secure title insurance and still transfer the title.

Who can perform a real estate closing?

As determined by state law, real estate closings are conducted by attorneys in Alabama. However, corporate real estate closing can be conducted internally.

Who can prepare real estate closing documents?

The closing documents can be drawn up by the closing attorney or by the buyer and seller. However, an attorney must oversee the closing itself.

How can a title be conveyed?

Title can be transferred through each of the common law conveyances. They are joint tenancy, tenancy in common, and tenancy by the entirety. Because this is not a community property state, title may not be held as community property.

What are the documentary or transfer taxes and fees?

Alabama charges a documentary or transfer fee. The name of the tax varies by municipality. It is based on the appraised value of the property and not the sale price. There is a title-recording fee of $2 for each page.

Are closing costs open to negotiation?

Closing costs can be negotiated in Alabama, but each lender will decide independently which costs will be negotiated, if any.

What are the mortgage taxes?

Alabama does charge a mortgage tax of $1.50 for each $1,000 borrowed.

How is the mortgage secured?

In Alabama a mortgage is secured with a warranty deed or with a quitclaim deed.

Is there a redemption period after the sale?

Real estate transactions, including foreclosures, have a redemption period of one year.

How is a mortgage lien cancelled?

Liens are cancelled through a legal document called a satisfaction. Titles are cleared by an attorney.

For how long are judgment liens in effect?

Judgment liens expire and must be renewed by a court of law every 10 years. If the lien is not renewed it becomes void.

Can property taxes be paid in installments?

No. The amount due is determined by October 1 of each year and the tax is due by the following October 1.

Is this a community property state?

Alabama is not a community property state; therefore, titles cannot be held as community property. Married people may hold titles as sole and separate property without consent of spouses. Spousal rights are not assumed.

Are title insurance agents regulated?

Title agents are not regulated. Additionally, title insurers and their rates are not regulated, meaning that title insurance rates are open to free market competition and buyers would be well served to shop around.

What is the foreclosure process?

In accordance with state law, a foreclosure must take at least three weeks. The notice of foreclosure must be posted at least once a week for three weeks. After the foreclosure sale, the buyer faces a one-year redemption period. The foreclosure process can be carried out by the lender without the assistance or permission of a court. However, foreclosure can be carried out as a court order.

Who pays closing costs?

The state has no policy regarding who will pay closing costs. The buyer and seller are free to negotiate their own terms; however, the tradition is a 50-50 split.

Who handles consumer complaints?

Complaints are handled by the Alabama Real Estate Commission at 334-242-5544 or **www.arec.state.al.us**. Hearing impaired persons may call 334-396-0064.

Section 8.02: ALASKA

Land titles are checked how far back into the past?

Titles are researched back to the last titleholder. Of course, a buyer can request additional research.

Who can perform a real estate closing?

Closings can be conducted by an escrow agent, a bank mortgage broker, or an attorney.

Who can prepare real estate closing documents?

The closing documents can be drawn up by the closing attorney or by the buyer and seller. However, an attorney must oversee the closing itself.

How can a title be conveyed?

In Alaska, title is passed by the signing of the deed by the current owner, followed by physically passing it to the new owner. When the new owner takes possession of the deed ownership is legally transferred. The transfer must be recorded at the recorder's office. Title can be transferred through each of the common law conveyances. They are joint tenancy, tenancy in common, and tenancy by the entirety. This is a community property state; title may be held as community property.

What are the documentary or transfer taxes and fees?

There are no documentary or transfer taxes. However, there is a recording fee of $15.00 for the first page and $3.00 for each additional page.

Are closing costs open to negotiation?

The closing fees are paid by both parties and can be negotiated. The state does not have a precedent for splitting these fees.

What are the mortgage taxes?

Alaska does not charge mortgage taxes.

How is the mortgage secured?

Mortgages are secured by a deed of trust. The foreclosure is limited to the deed of trust unless the lender states otherwise in the mortgage documents in which case, the borrower will owe the lender after the foreclosure if the foreclosure does not cover the entire debt.

Is there a redemption period after the sale?

Real estate transactions, including foreclosures, have a redemption period of one year.

How is a mortgage lien cancelled?

Liens are cancelled through a legal document called a deed of reconveyance. Titles are cleared by an attorney.

For how long are judgment liens in effect?

Judgment liens expire and must be renewed after five years. However, a lien will appear on the tile for 10 years even if it was not renewed after the initial five-year term.

Can property taxes be paid in installments?

Taxes can be paid in installments, traditionally of 15 percent at a time with interest. However, the percentages vary by municipality. The date taxes are levied and the due date will also vary by municipality.

Is this a community property state?

This is a community property state. Title may be held as community property. A spouse is considered to be a 50 percent owner unless he or she has waived these rights. Because Alaska is a community property state, the spouse is granted inheritance rights. The reader should know that Alaska has an opt-in clause in its community property law, meaning the estate must be set up as community property. Otherwise, the community property laws are not applicable.

Are title insurance agents regulated?

Title insurance agents are regulated by the state and their fees are subject to state approval. However, a state fee schedule does not exist.

What is the foreclosure process?

In accordance with state law, a foreclosure must take at least 90 days, but may not take more than 120 days. After the foreclosure sale, the buyer faces a one-year redemption period. The foreclosure process can be carried out by the lender without the assistance or permission of a court. However, foreclosure can be carried out as a court order.

Who pays closing costs?

Traditionally, the buyer and seller split closing costs 50-50.

Who handles consumer complaints?

1) Department of Community and Economic Development at 907-465-2521 or for TTY at 907-465-5437. 2) Department of Community and Economic Development, Insurance Division at 907-465-2521 or for TTY at 907-465-5437. 3) Division of Occupational Licensing Real Estate Commission at 907-269-8160.

Section 8.03: ARIZONA

Land titles are checked how far back into the past?

Titles are researched back to their source, usually a quitclaim deed.

Who can perform a real estate closing?

Escrow agents conduct closings. However, an attorney can oversee the closing if the buyer and seller wish.

Who can prepare real estate closing documents?

Closing documents can be prepared by an escrow agent, an attorney, or a real estate agent.

How can a title be conveyed?

Title is passed by warranty deed. Titles can be transferred through each of the common law conveyances. They are joint tenancy, tenancy-in-common, and tenancy by the entirety. Ownership has not passed until the deed has been recorded. Ownership can be taken through adverse possession with a minimum requirement of 10 years.

What are the documentary or transfer taxes and fees?

Documentary and transfer taxes are a flat rate of $2. Fees are $10 to $14.

Are closing costs open to negotiation?

Closing costs are not negotiable.

What are the mortgage taxes?

Arizona does not assess mortgage taxes.

How is the mortgage secured?

Mortgages are secured by a deed trust.

Is there a redemption period after the sale?

There is no redemption period. All sales are final. However, the state grants a builder's warranty with a maximum claim of $20,000.

How is a mortgage lien cancelled?

Liens are cancelled through a deed of release and a reconveyance. Titles are cleared by an attorney.

For how long are judgment liens in effect?

Liens expire after five years but may be renewed indefinitely every five years.

Can property taxes be paid in installments?

These taxes are assessed and due twice a year on November 1 and May 1. They can be paid in installments with interest.

Is this a community property state?

Yes. Title may be held as community property. A spouse is considered to be a 50 percent owner unless she or he has waived these rights. Because Arizona is a community property state, the spouse is granted inheritance rights.

Are title insurance agents regulated?

Title insurance agents and their fees are regulated by the Department of Insurance and the Department of Banking.

What is the foreclosure process?

In accordance with state law, a foreclosure must take at least 90 days. The foreclosure process is carried out by the lender without the assistance or permission of a court. However, foreclosure can be carried out as a court order.

Who pays closing costs?

Buyers and sellers are free to split closing costs as they wish. A 50-50 split is traditional.

Who handles consumer complaints?

1) State Banking Department, 602-255-4421, **www.azbanking.com.**

2) Department of Insurance, 800-325-2548, **www.state.az.us.**

3) Department of Real Estate, 602-468-1414 ext. 100, **www.re.state. az.us.**

Section 8.04: ARKANSAS

Land titles are checked how far back into the past?

Titles are researched back 40 years or back to the creation.

Who can perform a real estate closing?

Escrow agents, title companies, and attorneys conduct closings.

Who can prepare real estate closing documents?

The closing documents must be prepared by an attorney.

How can a title be conveyed?

Title can be transferred by a warranty deed, quitclaim deed, or a special warranty deed. However, the document must have a grantor, grantee, a description of the property, the signature of the grantor, and acknowledgement of acceptance. Title can be transferred through each of the common law conveyances. They are joint tenancy, tenancy in common, and tenancy by the entirety.

What are the documentary or transfer taxes and fees?

Transfer taxes are $3.30 for the first $100.000, usually split by the buyer and seller. There is a recording fee of $4 for the first page and $2 for each additional page, and a clerk fee of $1.

Are closing costs open to negotiation?

Closing costs are negotiable.

What are the mortgage taxes?

Arkansas does not assess mortgage taxes.

How is the mortgage secured?

Mortgages are secured by a deed of trust.

Is there a redemption period after the sale?

There is no redemption period. All sales are final. The state does not grant a builder's warranty.

How is a mortgage lien cancelled?

Liens are cancelled through a release deed and a marginal record entry reserving the lien. Titles are cleared by an attorney.

For how long are judgment liens in effect?

Liens expire after 10 years but can be renewed.

Can property taxes be paid in installments?

Taxes are assessed and levied from the third Monday in February through October 10. They can be paid in quarterly installments due in March and November. Quarterly installments are considered delinquent after October 10.

Is this a community property state?

No. Therefore, titles cannot be held as community property. Married people may hold titles as sole and separate property without consent of spouses. Spousal rights are not assumed.

Are title insurance agents regulated?

Title insurance agents must be licensed, but if the agent is an attorney, a license is not required. Their fees are not regulated.

What is the foreclosure process?

The foreclosure process is carried out by court order only and does not carry a minimum time limit.

Who pays closing costs?

Each party pays their own closing cost. The buyer pays the lender's title insurance policy premium.

Who handles consumer complaints?

1) State Banking Department, 501-324-9019, **www.state.ar.us/bank.**

2) Department of Insurance, 800-282-9134, **www.state.ar.us/insurance**. 3) Real Estate Commission, 501-683-8010, **www.state.ar.us/arec/arecweb.html**.

Section 8.05: CALIFORNIA

Land titles are checked how far back into the past?

Titles are researched back to the last titleholder. Of course, a buyer can request additional research.

Who can perform a real estate closing?

Escrow agents conduct closings. However, large transactions are overseen by an attorney.

Who can prepare real estate closing documents?

The closing documents can be prepared by the escrow division of a title company, an escrow agent or an attorney.

How can a title be conveyed?

Titles are conveyed by grant deed. The document must have a

grantor, grantee, a description of the property, the signature of the grantor, and acknowledgement of acceptance. Title can be transferred through each of the common law conveyances. They are joint tenancy, tenancy in common, tenancy by the entirety, and as community property.

What are the documentary or transfer taxes and fees?

The transfer tax is $1.10 for every $1,000. Additional city or county transfer taxes may apply. The recording fee is $7 for the first page and $3 for each additional page.

Are closing costs open to negotiation?

Closing fees are not negotiable.

What are the mortgage taxes?

California does not assess mortgage taxes.

How is the mortgage secured?

Mortgages are secured through a deed of trust.

Is there a redemption period after the sale?

California does not have a sale redemption period unless it is a tax foreclosure sale.

How is a mortgage lien cancelled?

Liens are cancelled through a deed of reconveyance. Titles are cleared by an attorney.

For how long are judgment liens in effect?

Judgment liens expire after 10 years unless they are renewed.

Can property taxes be paid in installments?

Taxes are assessed and levied once each year on November 1, but can be paid in two installments on November 1 and February 1.

Is this a community property state?

Yes. Title may be held as community property. A spouse is considered to be a 50 percent owner unless she or he has waived these rights. Because California is a community property state, the spouse is granted inheritance rights.

Are title insurance agents regulated?

Agents and their fees are regulated by the Department of Insurance.

What is the foreclosure process?

The borrower has three months to catch up on the debt after the notice of foreclosure has been issued. If the borrower fails to remedy the default within three months, the property can be sold at an auction with or without a court order.

Who pays closing costs?

It varies by county. Most southern counties split the fees 50-50. Many northern counties split them with the seller paying 75 percent and the buyer paying 25 percent.

Who handles consumer complaints?

1) Department of Corporations (for escrow complaints), 800-622-0620, **www.corp.ca.gov**. 2) Insurance Commissioner, Department of Insurance, 916-492-3500, **www.insurance.ca.gov**. 3) Department of Real Estate, 916-227-0931, **www.dre.ca.gov**.

Section 8.06: COLORADO

Land titles are checked how far back into the past?

The title search varies greatly depending on the intended use of the land.

Who can perform a real estate closing?

Escrow agents, title companies, and attorneys conduct closings.

Who can prepare real estate closing documents?

The closing documents can be prepared only by an attorney or a real estate agent who has been licensed by the Real Estate Commission.

How can a title be conveyed?

The title is passed through a warranty deed and special warranty deed for commercial real estate. Titles can be transferred through each of the common law conveyances. They are joint tenancy, tenancy in common, and tenancy by the entirety.

What are the documentary or transfer taxes and fees?

The transfer tax is $14 for each $1,000. The recording fee is $ 6 per page. Lien releases are $14 per page.

Are closing costs open to negotiation?

Closing costs cannot be negotiated.

What are the mortgage taxes?

Colorado does not charge a mortgage tax.

How is the mortgage secured?

Mortgages are secured through a deed of trust. Special legal protections are given to sellers who finance part of the sale for the buyer.

Is there a redemption period after the sale?

Real estate transactions, including foreclosures, have a redemption period of 45 days.

How is a mortgage lien cancelled?

Liens are cancelled through a legal document called a release. Titles are cleared by an attorney.

For how long are judgment liens in effect?

Liens expire after six years unless they are renewed.

Can property taxes be paid in installments?

Taxes are assessed and levied each year on January 1 and are due by June 1. However, they can be paid in two installments on February 28 and April 30.

Is this a community property state?

Officially, Colorado is not a community property state. However, it has some community property statutes.

Are title insurance agents regulated?

Title agents and their fees are regulated by the State Department of Insurance.

What is the foreclosure process?

The foreclosure process is carried out by court order only. However, the lender can conduct a foreclosure without a court order if ownership involves a deed of trust and a public trustee. The process allows the owner a minimum of either three or four months to circumvent foreclosure.

Who pays closing costs?

Traditionally, closing costs are divided 50-50 between the buyer and seller.

Who handles consumer complaints?

1) Department of Regulatory Agencies, Division of Banking, 303-894-7575, **www.dora.state.co.us/banking**. 2) Commissioner, Division of Insurance, 303-894-7499 ext. 4311, **www.dora.state.co.us/insurance**. 3) Department of Regulatory Agencies, Division of Real Estate, 303-894-2166, **www.dors.state.co.us/real-estate**.

Section 8.07: CONNECTICUT

Land titles are checked how far back into the past?

Titles are researched at least 40 years into the past. Otherwise, the title is not considered marketable.

Who can perform a real estate closing?

Closings are always conducted by an attorney.

Who can prepare real estate closing documents?

The closing documents must be prepared by an attorney.

How can a title be conveyed?

Title is passed by warranty deed or by a quitclaim deed. Titles can be transferred through each of the common law conveyances. They are joint tenancy, tenancy in common, and tenancy by the entirety. Titles cannot be held as community property. Married people may hold titles as sole and separate property without consent of spouses. Spousal rights are not assumed.

What are the documentary or transfer taxes and fees?

The transfer taxes are $1.10 for each $1,000. The state assesses a separate fee that varies. The recording fee is $15 for the first page and $5 for each additional page.

Are closing costs open to negotiation?

Closing costs can be negotiated between the buyer and seller.

What are the mortgage taxes?

This state does not levy mortgage taxes.

How is the mortgage secured?

Mortgages are secured through the promissory note.

Is there a redemption period after the sale?

No. All sales are final.

How is a mortgage lien cancelled?

Liens are cancelled through a legal document called a release of mortgage. Titles are cleared by an attorney.

For how long are judgment liens in effect?

Judgment liens are effective for 20 years unless they are renewed by a court.

Can property taxes be paid in installments?

Taxes are assessed and levied once each year on July 1. The due date depends on the local town, but may be annually, semi-annually, or quarterly. Installment payments can be made at 1.5 percent interest.

Is this a community property state?

Connecticut is not a community property state. Therefore, titles cannot be held as community property. Married people may hold titles as sole and separate property without consent of spouses. Spousal rights are not assumed.

Are title insurance agents regulated?

Title insurance agents must be attorneys who hold a bar license in Connecticut. Their insurance rates must be filed with the Insurance Commissioner.

What is the foreclosure process?

Foreclosure is only by court order. They take two forms, suit in equity and strict foreclosure. Strict foreclosure does allow period of three to six months if allowed by the court. However, suit in equity does not allow for a redemption period. The foreclosure is final after the sale.

Who pays closing costs?

Closing costs can be negotiated between the buyer and seller.

Who handles consumer complaints?

1) Consumer Credit Division, 800-831-7225, **www.state.ct.us/ dob/pages/ccdiv.htm**. 2) Consumer Affairs, 800-203-3447, **www.state.ct.us/cid**.

Section 8.08: DELAWARE

Land titles are checked how far back into the past?

Titles are researched 60 years into the past.

Who can perform a real estate closing?

Closings are always conducted by an attorney.

Who can prepare real estate closing documents?

Closing documents must be prepared by an attorney.

How can a title be conveyed?

Titles are transferred by warranty deed. The deed must include the following information: the grantor, the grantee, consideration, the words grant and convey, a description of the property, and the signature of the grantor. Title is passed when it is recorded. Title can be transferred through each of the common law conveyances. They are joint tenancy, tenancy in common, and tenancy by the entirety. However, tenancy in common is assumed unless the title states otherwise. The state does allow a joint tenancy with right of survivorship title. Titles cannot be held as community property. Married people may hold titles as sole and separate property without consent of spouses. Spousal rights are not assumed. Adverse possession is allowed after 20 years.

What are the documentary or transfer taxes and fees?

The transfer tax is 3 percent of the sale. The recording fee is also 3 percent of the sale.

Are closing costs open to negotiation?

Closing costs are paid by the buyer.

What are the mortgage taxes?

Delaware does not levy mortgage taxes.

How is the mortgage secured?

Mortgages are secured through the promissory note.

Is there a redemption period after the sale?

All sales are final, except tax foreclosures, which allow a redemption period if it is provided by a court.

How is a mortgage lien cancelled?

Liens are cancelled through a legal document called a mortgage satisfaction piece. Titles are cleared by an attorney.

For how long are judgment liens in effect?

Judgment liens are effective for 10 years. Renewals must be made by the plaintiff or the successor of the plaintiff.

Can property taxes be paid in installments?

Taxes are levied and assessed by each independent county. Times of assessment vary. However, the tax is always due by August 31 of each year. Unless a special court arrangement is made, property owners cannot make installment payments on their taxes.

Is this a community property state?

This is not a community property state.

Are title insurance agents regulated?

Agents are regulated by the Insurance Commissioner. Their rates must be recorded with the commissioner. However, rates are not regulated.

What is the foreclosure process?

Foreclosure is only by court order. The foreclosure process must take a minimum of 120 or 150 days. The foreclosure sale is final unless the court specifies otherwise.

Who pays closing costs?

Closing costs are paid by the buyer.

Who handles consumer complaints?

1) Office of the Bank Commissioner, Compliance Staff, 302-739-4235, **www.state.de.us/bank**. 2) Department of Insurance, 800-282-8611, **www.state.de.us/inscom**. 3) Real Estate Commission, 302-739-4522, **www.professionallicensing.state.de.us/boards/realestate/index. shtml**.

Section 8.09: DISTRICT OF COLUMBIA

Land titles are checked how far back into the past?

Titles are researched 60 years into the past.

Who can perform a real estate closing?

Closings can be conveyed by a title insurance company or an attorney.

Who can prepare real estate closing documents?

Closing documents can be prepared by a title insurance company, a settlement company, the agents of an attorney, or an attorney.

How can a title be conveyed?

Titles are passed by special warranty deed. The specifics of the title are meticulously spelled out by the law. Refer to D.C. Code Ann. §§45-501, 45-801 and 45-803 (1990). Title can be transferred through each of the common law conveyances. They are joint tenancy, tenancy in common, and tenancy by the entirety. Titles cannot be held as community property. Married people may hold titles as sole and separate property without consent of spouses. Spousal rights are not assumed. Adverse possession is allowed after 15 years or 20 years if the owner has a physical disability.

What are the documentary or transfer taxes and fees?

The transfer tax is 1.1 percent of the sale. Recording fees are $15 for the first two pages and $5 for each additional page. There is a recording tax of 1.1 percent of the sale.

Are closing costs open to negotiation?

Closing costs are paid by the buyer. The transfer tax is paid by the seller.

What are the mortgage taxes?

The mortgage tax is 1.1 percent of the appraised value of the deed of trust. Construction loans are also assessed a 1.1 percent tax.

How is the mortgage secured?

Mortgages are secured with a deed of trust.

Is there a redemption period after the sale?

No. All sales are final.

How is a mortgage lien cancelled?

Liens are cancelled through a legal document called a deed of release. Special legal protections are given to sellers who finance part of the buyer's purchase.

For how long are judgment liens in effect?

Judgment liens are indefinite.

Can property taxes be paid in installments?

Taxes are assessed and levied from October 1 through September 30 and are due either before September 15 or March 31. They can be paid in two installments with due dates of September 15 and March 21. A late payment penalty of 10 percent of the bill is added after the due date. Installment payments incur 1 percent per month interest.

Does the District of Columbia have community property status?

No.

Are title insurance agents regulated?

Title insurance agents are not regulated and neither are their fees.

What is the foreclosure process?

In accordance with state law, a foreclosure must take at least six weeks. A notice must be given to the owner 30 days before the sale date. The foreclosure process is carried out by the lender without the assistance or permission of a court. However, foreclosure can be carried out as a court order. The foreclosure does not have a redemption period.

Who pays closing costs?

Closing costs are paid by the buyer. The transfer tax is paid by the seller.

Who handles consumer complaints?

1) Department of Insurance and Securities Regulation, 202-727-8000.

Section 8.10: FLORIDA

Land titles are checked how far back into the past?

Titles are researched back to the patent of the U.S. government. Each document within the chain is checked back to its root title.

Who can perform a real estate closing?

Closings can be conveyed by an attorney, the title insurer, or a title agent.

Who can prepare real estate closing documents?

Closing documents must be prepared by an attorney holding a Florida bar license.

How can a title be conveyed?

Title is transferred by a statutory warranty deed. Refer to Fla. Stat.

ch. 689.02 (1983). The transfer must take place in the presence of two witnesses and a notary public. Title can be transferred through each of the common law conveyances. They are joint tenancy, tenancy in common, and tenancy by the entirety. Titles cannot be held as community property. Married people may hold titles as sole and separate property without consent of spouses. Spousal rights are not assumed.

What are the documentary or transfer taxes and fees?

The transfer tax is in the form of a documentary stamp that is assessed in the amount of $.70 for each $100. The recording fee is $6 for the first page and $4.50 for each additional page.

Are closing costs open to negotiation?

The party responsible for closing costs varies by jurisdiction.

What are the mortgage taxes?

The mortgage taxes are in the form of a documentary stamp. It is assessed at $.35 for each $100.

How is the mortgage secured?

The mortgage is secured by a promissory note.

Is there a redemption period after the sale?

The post-sale redemption period ends when the certificate of sale is issued.

How is a mortgage lien cancelled?

Liens are cancelled through a legal document called a satisfaction of mortgage or a release of mortgage. Special legal protections are given to sellers who finance part of the buyer's purchase.

For how long are judgment liens in effect?

Judgment liens are effective for 10 years. After 10 years the lien is renewed by refilling it with the recorder's office.

Can property taxes be paid in installments?

Taxes are assessed and levied on November 1 of each year. Installments are not accepted.

Is this a community property state?

No. However, a community property title can be held and recognized by the state if it is set up as one by the titleholders.

Are title insurance agents regulated?

Title agents that are not attorneys must be licensed. Otherwise, they are not regulated.

What is the foreclosure process?

Foreclosure is only by court order. The foreclosure process must take a minimum of three months. The redemption period ends when the certificate of sale is issued.

Who pays closing costs?

The party responsible for closing costs varies by jurisdiction.

Who handles consumer complaints?

1) Division of Financial Investigations, 800-848-3792, **www.dbf.state.flus**. 2) Department of Business and Professional Regulation, 407-423-6053, **www.state.fl.us**.

Section 8.11: GEORGIA

Land titles are checked how far back into the past?

Titles are researched 50 years into the past as per the state bar.

Who can perform a real estate closing?

Closings are conducted by attorneys.

Who can prepare real estate closing documents?

Closing documents can be prepared by attorneys or lenders.

How can a title be conveyed?

Title is conveyed through warranty deed or quit claim deed. Title can be transferred through each of the common law conveyances. They are joint tenancy, tenancy in common, and tenancy by the entirety. Titles cannot be held as community property. Married people may hold titles as sole and separate property without consent of spouses. Spousal rights are not assumed.

What are the documentary or transfer taxes and fees?

The transfer tax is $1 for each $1,000. The recording fee is $10 for the first page and $2 for each additional page.

Are closing costs open to negotiation?

The precedent is for closing costs to be paid by the buyer without negotiation.

What are the mortgage taxes?

The mortgage tax is $3 for each $1,000.

How is the mortgage secured?

Mortgages are secured with a deed.

Is there a redemption period after the sale?

No. All sales are final.

How is a mortgage lien cancelled?

Mortgage liens are cancelled by filing the original deed, used as collateral, with cancellation written across the front.

For how long are judgment liens in effect?

Judgment liens are effective for seven years. After seven years the creditor must file a new claim.

Can property taxes be paid in installments?

Taxes are assessed and levied on January 1 but are due at varying times depending on the municipality. Taxes can be paid in two installments if prior approval is obtained from the county. However, 12 percent interest will be imposed.

Is this a community property state?

No.

Are title insurance agents regulated?

Title insurance agents are not regulated and neither are their fees.

What is the foreclosure process?

In accordance with state law, a foreclosure must take at least four weeks. The sale must be advertised each week for four consecutive weeks. The sale must be advertised the first Tuesday of each month. The foreclosure process is carried out by the lender without the assistance or permission of a court. However, foreclosure can be carried out as a court order. The foreclosure does not have a redemption period.

Who pays closing costs?

The tradition is for closing costs to be paid by the buyer. However, sellers pay the transfer tax.

Who handles consumer complaints?

1) Department of Banking and Finance, 770-986-1633, **www.ganet. org/dbf/dbf.html**. 2) Georgia Real Estate Commission, 404-656-3916, **www.2.state.ga.us/ga.real_estate**. 3) Insurance and Safety Fire Commission, 800-656-2298, TDD/TTY 404-656-4031, **www. inscomm.state.ga.us**.

Section 8.12: HAWAII

Land titles are checked how far back into the past?

Titles are researched back to the previous title insurance.

Who can perform a real estate closing?

Traditionally, closings are conducted by an escrow agent.

Who can prepare real estate closing documents?

They do not dictate who may prepare the closing documents.

How can a title be conveyed?

Title is conveyed through warranty deed, quitclaim deed, deed and assignment of lease. Title can be transferred through each of the common law conveyances. They are joint tenancy, tenancy in common, and tenancy by the entirety. Titles cannot be held as community property. Married people may hold titles as sole and separate property without consent of spouses. Spousal rights are not assumed.

What are the documentary or transfer taxes and fees?

A conveyance tax of $.10 for each $100 is assessed. The recording fee is $20.

Are closing costs open to negotiation?

The payment of closing costs may be negotiated by the buyer and seller when the purchase contract is created.

What are the mortgage taxes?

Hawaii does not levy mortgage taxes.

How is the mortgage secured?

Mortgages are secured through the promissory note.

Is there a redemption period after the sale?

No. All sales are final.

How is a mortgage lien cancelled?

Mortgage liens are cancelled by filing a release of mortgage or satisfaction of mortgage.

For how long are judgment liens in effect?

Judgment liens are effective for 10 years. After 10 years they must be renewed.

Can property taxes be paid in installments?

Taxes are assessed and levied in two installments. The first is due by August 20. The second is due by February 20. An interest rate of 10 percent is imposed on late payments.

Is this a community property state?

Hawaii is not a community property state.

Are title insurance agents regulated?

Agents are regulated by the state. Their fees must be filed with the state and are published.

What is the foreclosure process?

The foreclosure process is usually carried out by a court. However, foreclosure can be carried out by a lender. Details of the process can be found at HAW. Rev. Stat. § 667 (1993). Foreclosures do not have a redemption period.

Who pays closing costs?

The precedent is for closing costs to be split 50-50 between the buyer and seller. However, parties may work out terms as they wish in the purchase contract.

Who handles consumer complaints?

1) Department of Commerce and Consumer Affairs, 808-586-2820, **www.state.hi.us/dcca/dfi**. 2) Department of Commerce and Consumer Affairs, Insurance Division, 808-586-2790, **www.state.hi.us/dcca/ins**.

Section 8.13: IDAHO

Land titles are checked how far back into the past?

Titles are researched to their original U.S. patents.

Who can perform a real estate closing?

Closings are conducted by title companies.

Who can prepare real estate closing documents?

Closing documents are prepared by attorneys. Some documents can be prepared by employees of the title company.

How can a title be conveyed?

Titles are conveyed by warranty deed, grant deed, and quit claim deed. Title can be transferred through each of the common law conveyances. They are joint tenancy, tenancy in common, and tenancy by the entirety. Titles can be held as community property. Married people may hold titles as sole and separate property only with the consent of their spouse. Spousal rights are assumed.

What are the documentary or transfer taxes and fees?

Idaho does not have a transfer tax. The recording fee is $3 per page.

Are closing costs open to negotiation?

Traditionally, closing costs are split between the buyer and seller without negotiation. However, different arrangements can be worked out when the purchase contract is created.

What are the mortgage taxes?

Idaho does not levy mortgage taxes.

How is the mortgage secured?

Mortgages are secured with a deed of trust that includes a power of sale.

Is there a redemption period after the sale?

No. All sales are final.

How is a mortgage lien cancelled?

Mortgage liens are cancelled by satisfaction or release of mortgage.

For how long are judgment liens in effect?

Judgment liens are effective for five years and must be renewed before expiration or they are void.

Can property taxes be paid in installments?

Taxes are levied and assessed once each year and due by the fourth Monday of November.

Is this a community property state?

Yes.

Are title insurance agents regulated?

Agents and their rates are regulated by the Department of Insurance.

What is the foreclosure process?

The foreclosure process is usually carried out by the lender. However, foreclosure can be carried out by court order. The process must take a minimum of 120 days. Foreclosures do not have a redemption period.

Who pays closing costs?

Traditionally, closing costs are split between the buyer and seller without negotiation.

Who handles consumer complaints?

1) Department of Finance, 208-332-8004. 2) Department of Insurance, 208-334-4250, **www.doi.state.id.us**. 3) Idaho Real Estate Commission, 208-334-3285.

Section 8.14: ILLINOIS

Land titles are checked how far back into the past?

Titles are researched back as far as the title insurance company deems necessary. This process is not regulated by the state.

Who can perform a real estate closing?

Closings are conducted by title companies.

Who can prepare real estate closing documents?

The closing documents are prepared by an attorney.

How can a title be conveyed?

Title is conveyed by warranty deed or quit claim deed. Title can be transferred through each of the common law conveyances. They are joint tenancy, tenancy in common, and tenancy by the entirety. Titles cannot be held as community property. Married people may hold titles as sole and separate property without consent of spouses. Spousal rights are not assumed.

What are the documentary or transfer taxes and fees?

Each municipality levies its own transfer tax that will vary. However, the state levies a transfer tax of $1 per $1,000 as well as a county tax of $.50 per $1,000. The recording fee is $12 for the first four pages and $1 for each additional page.

Are closing costs open to negotiation?

Costs are traditionally paid by the buyer. The transfer tax is paid by the seller. However, it can be negotiated during the creation of the purchase contract.

What are the mortgage taxes?

Illinois does not have a mortgage tax.

How is the mortgage secured?

Mortgages are secured with a promissory note.

Is there a redemption period after the sale?

No. All sales are final.

How is a mortgage lien cancelled?

Mortgage liens are cancelled by release.

For how long are judgment liens in effect?

Judgment liens are effective for seven years.

Can property taxes be paid in installments?

Taxes are levied and assessed in two yearly installments. Installments are due before June 1. and September 1. In Cook County installments are due before March 1 and August 1. Debtors cannot get additional installments. However, 1.5 percent interest is added to late tax payments each month.

Is this a community property state?

Illinois is not a community property state.

Are title insurance agents regulated?

Agents must register with the state but are not licensed. Their fees are not regulated.

What is the foreclosure process?

The process is usually carried through a court order. The process must take a minimum of one month, but the judicial process takes one year. Foreclosures do have a redemption period.

Who pays closing costs?

Costs are traditionally paid by the buyer or split 50-50 between the buyer and seller. The transfer tax and the title insurance premium are paid by the seller.

Who handles consumer complaints?

1) Office of Banks and Real Estate, 877-793-3470, TDD 217-524-6644.
2) Department of Insurance, 217-782-4515, TDD 217-524-4872, **www. state.il.us/ins/**.

Section 8.15: INDIANA

Land titles are checked how far back into the past?

Titles are researched back as far as the title insurance company deems necessary. This process is not regulated by the state.

Who can perform a real estate closing?

Anyone can conduct a closing.

Who can prepare real estate closing documents?

Anyone can prepare the closing documents.

How can a title be conveyed?

Title can be conveyed through a warranty deed. Title can be transferred through each of the common law conveyances. They are joint tenancy, tenancy in common, and tenancy by the entirety. Titles cannot be held as community property. Married people may hold titles as sole and separate property without consent of spouses. Spousal rights are not assumed.

What are the documentary or transfer taxes and fees?

The transfer taxes are from $1 to $3 for each transaction, but all counties do not charge them. Recording fees vary by county. The charge is usually $12.

Are closing costs open to negotiation?

Closing costs are negotiable if the lender is willing to negotiate.

What are the mortgage taxes?

Indiana does not levy mortgage taxes.

How is the mortgage secured?

Mortgages are secured with a promissory note.

Is there a redemption period after the sale?

No. All sales are final.

How is a mortgage lien cancelled?

Mortgage liens are cancelled through the recording of a release.

For how long are judgment liens in effect?

Judgment liens are effective for 10 years and cannot be renewed.

Can property taxes be paid in installments?

Taxes are levied and assessed once each year and are due by March 1. They can be paid in two installments due by May 10 and November 10. Interest is not charged on installments.

Is this a community property state?

No.

Are title insurance agents regulated?

Title agents are not regulated and neither are their rates.

What is the foreclosure process?

Foreclosure is only by court order. The process must take a minimum of three months. The redemption period ends when the Sheriff's Deed is issued.

Who pays closing costs?

The buyer usually pays closing costs and the lender pays for title insurance premium. The seller pays the title insurance premium for the buyer's policy.

Who handles consumer complaints?

Complaints can be filed with the following agencies.

1) Department of Financial Institutions, 317-232-3955, **www.dfi.state.in.us**. 2) Department of Insurance, 317-232-2385, **www.state.in.us/idoi**.

Section 8.16: IOWA

Land titles are checked how far back into the past?

Titles are researched at least 40 years into the past in accordance with state law.

Who can perform a real estate closing?

Closings are conducted by attorneys and real estate agents.

Who can prepare real estate closing documents?

Closing documents are prepared by attorneys and real estate agents.

How can a title be conveyed?

Title is conveyed by warranty deed. Title can be transferred through each of the common law conveyances. They are joint tenancy, tenancy in common, and tenancy by the entirety. Titles cannot be held as community property. Married people may hold titles as sole and separate property without consent of spouses. Spousal rights are not assumed.

What are the documentary or transfer taxes and fees?

The transfer tax is $1.60 for each $1,000. The recording fee is $1 per documents and $5 per page.

Are closing costs open to negotiation?

Closing costs are not negotiable. However, you may negotiate which party pays them.

What are the mortgage taxes?

Iowa does not levy mortgages taxes.

How is the mortgage secured?

Mortgages are secured with a deed of trust.

Is there a redemption period after the sale?

The post-sale redemption period varies from one county to the next.

How is a mortgage lien cancelled?

Mortgage liens are cancelled through a mortgage release.

For how long are judgment liens in effect?

Judgment liens expire every 10 years, but can be renewed.

Can property taxes be paid in installments?

Taxes are levied and assessed once each year on September 1 and are due on either September 1 or March 1. They can be paid in two installments due before September 1. and March 1. However, 1.5 percent interest per month is added to installment payments.

Is this a community property state?

No.

Are title insurance agents regulated?

Agents are not regulated and neither are their fees.

What is the foreclosure process?

The foreclosure process is usually carried through a court order. However, a lender can conduct a foreclosure. The process must take a minimum of two months. Foreclosures have a redemption period that varies from one county to the next.

Who pays closing costs?

Who pays closing costs is negotiable and can be worked out when the purchase contract is created.

Who handles consumer complaints?

1) Department of Commerce, 515-281-4014, **www.idob.state.ia.us/**. 2) Insurance Division, 877-955-1212, **www.iid.state.ia.us/**. 3) Professional Licensing and Regulation Division, Iowa Real Estate Commission, 515-281-7393, **www.state.ia.us/government/com/**.

Section 8.17: KANSAS

Land titles are checked how far back into the past?

Titles are researched back to their U.S. patents. Those conducting searches must be licensed. The licensing process involves competency testing and is strict. Titles involving Indian lands must be presented before the Indian Commission.

Who can perform a real estate closing?

Closings are conducted by title companies, lenders, real estate agents, and escrow agents.

Who can prepare real estate closing documents?

They are prepared by title companies, attorneys, and lenders.

How can a title be conveyed?

Title is conveyed through warranty deed only. Title can be transferred through each of the common law conveyances. They are joint tenancy, tenancy in common, and tenancy by the entirety. Titles cannot be held as community property. Married people may hold titles as sole and separate property without consent of spouses. Spousal rights are not assumed.

What are the documentary or transfer taxes and fees?

Kansas does not levy transfer taxes. The recording fee is $6 for the first page and $2 for each additional page.

Are closing costs open to negotiation?

How the costs are split can be negotiated. However, the precedent is a 50-50 split between the buyer and seller.

What are the mortgage taxes?

Kansas levies a mortgage tax of $2 for each $1,000 mortgaged.

How is the mortgage secured?

Mortgages are secured through a promissory note.

Is there a redemption period after the sale?

Sales have a six-month redemption period including foreclosures.

How is a mortgage lien cancelled?

Mortgage liens are cancelled through a release or satisfaction of mortgage.

For how long are judgment liens in effect?

Judgment liens are effective for five years. Afterwards, they can be renewed twice for two-year periods. With the renewals, judgment liens can be in effect for up to seven years.

Can property taxes be paid in installments?

Kansas assesses and levies taxes from January 1 through December 31. Taxes can be paid in two installments. However, 1.8 percent per month interest is added to the installments.

Is this a community property state?

No.

Are title insurance agents regulated?

Agents are regulated by the Insurance Commissioner's Office. Their fees must be recorded at the same office.

What is the foreclosure process?

The foreclosure process is usually carried through a court order. However, a lender can conduct a foreclosure. The process must take a minimum of 90 to 120 days. Foreclosures have a redemption period of six months.

Who pays closing costs?

The precedent is a 50-50 split between the buyer and seller.

Who handles consumer complaints?

1) Kansas Real Estate Commission, 785-296-3411, **www.accesskansas.org/krec**. 2) Insurance Department, 800-432-2484, **www.ksinsurance.org**.

Section 8.18: KENTUCKY

Land titles are checked how far back into the past?

Titles are researched either 40 or 60 years, varying by insurer.

Who can perform a real estate closing?

Closings are conducted by an attorney.

Who can prepare real estate closing documents?

The closing documents are prepared by an attorney. The seller can prepare the deed.

How can a title be conveyed?

Title is conveyed through grant deed and bargain-and-sale deed. Title can be transferred through each of the common law conveyances. They are joint tenancy, tenancy in common, and tenancy by the entirety. Titles cannot be held as community property. Married people may hold titles as sole and separate property without consent of spouses. Spousal rights are not assumed.

What are the documentary or transfer taxes and fees?

Transfer tax is $1 for each $1,000 of the sale price. Recording fee is $12 for the first three pages and $2 for each additional page.

Are closing costs open to negotiation?

Who pays closing costs is negotiable. However, the custom is for buyers to pay closing fees. Sellers pay for the deed preparation and the transfer tax.

What are the mortgage taxes?

Kentucky does not levy a mortgage tax.

How is the mortgage secured?

Mortgages are secured with a promissory note because deeds of trust do not offer foreclosure rights.

Is there a redemption period after the sale?

Kentucky offers a one-year redemption period after the sale, including foreclosures. However, there are statutory restrictions.

How is a mortgage lien cancelled?

Mortgage liens are cancelled through a release.

For how long are judgment liens in effect?

Judgment liens are effective for 15 years but can be renewed indefinitely.

Can property taxes be paid in installments?

Taxes are levied and assessed once a year in October and are due by December 31. However, cities levy their own taxes that run on varying schedules. These taxes cannot be paid in installments.

Is this a community property state?

No.

Are title insurance agents regulated?

Agents and the fees they charge are not regulated.

What is the foreclosure process?

The foreclosure process is usually carried through a court order. However, a lender can conduct a foreclosure. The process must take a minimum of three months. Foreclosures have a redemption period of one year.

Who pays closing costs?

The custom is for buyers to pay closing fees. Sellers pay for the deed preparation and the transfer tax.

Who handles consumer complaints?

1) Department of Financial Institutions, 502-573-3390, **www.dfi.state.ky.us/**. 2) Department of Insurance, 800-595-6053, **www.doi.state.ky.us/**. 3) Real Estate Commission, 502-425-4273, **www.krec.ky.gov**.

Section 8.19: LOUISIANA

Land titles are checked how far back into the past?

Titles are researched back 49 years if they are for commercial property and 35 years if they are for residential property.

Who can perform a real estate closing?

Closings can be conducted by a notary public or an attorney.

Who can prepare real estate closing documents?

A notary public or the staff of the notary public can prepare them.

How can a title be conveyed?

Title is conveyed by warranty deed or by the act of sale itself. However, the sale must contain certain actions to transfer the title. Refer to La. Civ. Code Ann. Art. 1839 (West 1987). Title can be transferred through each of the common law conveyances. They are joint tenancy, tenancy in common, and tenancy by the entirety. Titles can be held as community property. Married people may hold titles as sole and separate property, but only with consent of spouses. Spousal rights are assumed. Bad-faith adverse possession is permitted after 30 years. Good-faith adverse possession is permitted after 10 years. Special protections are given to sellers who finance part of the sale for the buyer.

What are the documentary or transfer taxes and fees?

Transfer taxes are $325 for residential property. All other transactions and recording fees are $325 for the first 10 pages and $100 for each additional page, not to exceed $2,500. Additional fees vary from one parish to another.

Are closing costs open to negotiation?

Who pays closing costs is open to negotiation when the purchase contract is created. However, the fees are usually paid by the buyer.

What are the mortgage taxes?

Louisiana does not levy mortgage taxes.

How is the mortgage secured?

Mortgages are secured through a promissory note.

Is there a redemption period after the sale?

No redemption is permitted after the sale. All sales are final. Statute La. Rev. Stat. Ann. § 9:3144 (West 1997, Supp. 1999) provides a one-year builder's warranty that the structure will be free from code violations. It also provides a two-year warranty for the plumbing, electrical, heating, cooling, and ventilation systems. The structure is guaranteed against structure defects due to code non-compliance for 10 years.

How is a mortgage lien cancelled?

The original promissory note must be filed with the clerk of court. If the original note is lost, the notary public, who lost the note, or the last holder of the note must file an affidavit with the clerk of court. An affidavit stating payment has been made in full must also be submitted by the creditor or the attorney of the debtor.

For how long are judgment liens in effect?

Judgment liens are in effect for 10 years. They must be renewed every 10 years.

Can property taxes be paid in installments?

Taxes are levied and assessed annually. They are due either December 31 or January 1. Taxes must be paid in full or penalties are added. Louisiana does not allow installment payments.

Is this a community property state?

Yes.

Are title insurance agents regulated?

Agents are regulated through the Louisiana Insurance Code. Fee must be filed with the commissioner of insurance.

What is the foreclosure process?

The foreclosure process is usually carried through a court order. The process must take a minimum of 120 days. The buyer must pay the property tax owed when the sale takes place. Foreclosures do not have a redemption period.

Who pays closing costs?

Usually the buyer will pay all closing costs.

Who handles consumer complaints?

1) Office of Financial Institutions, 225-925-4660, www.ofi.state.la.us/. 2) Department of Insurance, 800-259-5300, www.ldi.state.la.us. 3) Real Estate Commission, 504-925-4771.

Section 8.20: MAINE

Land titles are checked how far back into the past?

Titles must be researched back 40 years or to the last warranty deed in accordance with Maine Title Standards.

Who can perform a real estate closing?

Closings are be performed by attorneys.

Who can prepare real estate closing documents?

The closing documents are prepared by an attorney.

How can a title be conveyed?

Residential titles are conveyed by a warranty deed. Commercial titles are conveyed through a quitclaim deed. Title can be transferred through each of the common law conveyances. They are joint tenancy, tenancy in common, and tenancy by the entirety. Titles cannot be held as community property. Married people may hold titles as sole and separate property without consent of spouses. Spousal rights are not assumed.

What are the documentary or transfer taxes and fees?

The transfer taxes are $4 for each $1,000. The recording fee is $8 for the first page and $2 for each additional page.

Are closing costs open to negotiation?

Who pays closing costs can be negotiated. The fees are usually paid by the buyer.

What are the mortgage taxes?

Maine does not levy mortgage taxes.

How is the mortgage secured?

Mortgages are secured through a promissory note.

Is there a redemption period after the sale?

Maine provides a 90-day post-sale redemption period. Foreclosures have a six-month redemption period.

How is a mortgage lien cancelled?

Mortgage liens are cancelled through a discharge of mortgage.

For how long are judgment liens in effect?

Judgment liens are in effect for 20 years and cannot be renewed.

Can property taxes be paid in installments?

Taxes are assessed on April 1 of each year. However, they are levied by each independent municipality and due dates vary accordingly. They can be paid in two installments. Due dates and interest rate imposed depend on the municipality.

Is this a community property state?

No.

Are title insurance agents regulated?

Agents and their fees are regulated by the Maine Bureau of Insurance.

What is the foreclosure process?

Foreclosure is only by court order. The foreclosure process must take a minimum of six months. The redemption period is six months.

Who pays closing costs?

The fees are usually paid by the buyer.

Who handles consumer complaints?

Complaints can be filed with the following agencies.

1) Bureau of Insurance, 207-624-8475, **www.state.me.us/pfr/ins/ins_ index.htm**. 2) Department of Professional and Financial Regulation, 207-624-8527, **http://www.maine.gov/pfr/index.shtml**.

Section 8.21: MARYLAND

Land titles are checked how far back into the past?

Titles are researched back 60 years in accordance with state statutes.

Who can perform a real estate closing?

Closings are conducted by title companies and attorneys.

Who can prepare real estate closing documents?

Closing documents are prepared by title companies and attorneys.

How can a title be conveyed?

Title is conveyed through grant deed with the consideration stated on the deed. Title can be transferred through each of the common law conveyances. They are joint tenancy, tenancy in common, and tenancy by the entirety. Titles cannot be held as community property. Married people may hold titles as sole and separate property without consent of spouses. Spousal rights are not assumed. Maryland allows for title to be taken through adverse possession. Refer to Md. Code Ann., Cts. & Jud. Proc. § 5-103 (1995).

What are the documentary or transfer taxes and fees?

Transfer taxes are one half of 1 percent of the sale price. The recording fee is $20 for the first nine pages and $75 for 10 or more pages.

Are closing costs open to negotiation?

Closing costs are negotiable. However, the precedent is for the buyer and seller to split the closing fees.

What are the mortgage taxes?

Mortgage taxes vary from by municipality. All municipalities charge by $500 increments.

How is the mortgage secured?

Mortgages are secured through a deed of trust.

Is there a redemption period after the sale?

Maryland does not provide a post-sale redemption period. Builder warranties are provided by state statute Md. Code Ann., Real Prop. §§ 10-601 and 10-610 (1988). Special statutory protections are given to sellers who finance part of the sale for the buyer. Refer to Md. Code Ann., Real Prop. § 7-104 (1988).

How is a mortgage lien cancelled?

Mortgage liens are cancelled through a release or certificate of satisfaction.

For how long are judgment liens in effect?

Judgment liens last for 12 years. They can be extended for an additional 12 years if a renewal is filed before the expiration of the previous lien.

Can property taxes be paid in installments?

Taxes are levied and assessed on July 1 and are due on October 1 of each year. Taxes cannot be paid in installments.

Is this a community property state?

No.

Are title insurance agents regulated?

Agents are regulated by the Department of Insurance. The agents' fees must be registered with the Department of Insurance but are not regulated.

What is the foreclosure process?

The foreclosure process is usually carried through a court order. However, a lender can conduct a foreclosure. Foreclosures do not have a redemption period.

Who pays closing costs?

The precedent is for the buyer and seller to split the closing fees.

Who handles consumer complaints?

1) Consumer Credit Unit, 410-230-6097, **www.dllr.state.md.us/ finance**. 2) Insurance Administration, 800-492-6116, TYY 800-735-2258, **www.mdinsurance.state.md.us**. 3) Real Estate Commission, 888-218-5925, **www.dllr.state.md.us/license/occprof/recomm.html**.

Section 8.22: MASSACHUSETTS

Land titles are checked how far back into the past?

Titles are researched 50 years into the past as dictated by state statute.

Who can perform a real estate closing?

Closings are conducted by attorneys under the direction of the lender.

Who can prepare real estate closing documents?

The documents can be prepared by an attorney or a lender.

How can a title be conveyed?

Title is conveyed through warranty deed or quit claim deed. Title can be transferred through each of the common law conveyance. They are joint tenancy, tenancy in common, and tenancy by the entirety. Titles cannot be held as community property. Married people may hold titles as sole and separate property without consent of spouses. Spousal rights are not assumed.

What are the documentary or transfer taxes and fees?

Transfer taxes are $2.28 for each $500. However, a few counties charge $5.70 for each $1,000. Recording fee is either $45 or $60, depending on the county.

Are closing costs open to negotiation?

Buyers pay the closing and title insurance fees.

What are the mortgage taxes?

Massachusetts does not levy mortgage taxes.

How is the mortgage secured?

Mortgages are secured with a promissory note that allows power of sale in the event of default.

Is there a redemption period after the sale?

No.

How is a mortgage lien cancelled?

Mortgage liens are cancelled through a discharge.

For how long are judgment liens in effect?

Judgment liens are effective for six years and cannot be renewed.

Can property taxes be paid in installments?

Taxes are levied and assessed annually. Payments are due in quarterly or semi-quarterly installments. Quarterly installments are due on February 1, May 1, August 1, and November 1.

Is this a community property state?

No.

Are title insurance agents regulated?

Agents are not regulated and neither are their fees.

What is the foreclosure process?

The foreclosure process is usually carried out by the lender without the permission or oversight of a court. Foreclosures do not have a redemption period.

Who pays closing costs?

Buyers pay the closing and title insurance fees.

Who handles consumer complaints?

Complaints can be filed with the following agencies.

1) Office of Consumer Affairs, 617-521-7794, TYY 617-521-7490, **www.state.ma.us/doi**. 2) Board of Registration of Real Estate Brokers, 617-727-2373, TYY 617-727-2099, **www.state.ma.us/reg/boards/re**.

Section 8.23: MICHIGAN

Land titles are checked how far back into the past?

Titles are researched 40 years into the past.

Who can perform a real estate closing?

Closings are conducted by escrow agents.

Who can prepare real estate closing documents?

Closing documents are prepared by attorneys, mortgages brokers, or the parties involved in the transaction.

How can a title be conveyed?

Title is conveyed through warranty deed or quit claim deed that must state the consideration given. If the deed does not state the consideration, an affidavit stating the consideration must be attached. Title can be transferred through each of the common law conveyances. They are joint tenancy, tenancy in common, and tenancy by the entirety. Titles cannot be held as community property. Married people may hold titles as sole and separate property without consent of spouses. Spousal rights are not assumed.

What are the documentary or transfer taxes and fees?

Transfer taxes vary from county to county. Fees are all under

$1 and are charged for each $500 increment of the sale price. The recording fee is $5 for the first page and $2 for each additional page.

Are closing costs open to negotiation?

Buyers pay the closing fees and the title insurance premiums. The seller pays the transfer and recording fees by precedent.

What are the mortgage taxes?

Michigan does not levy mortgage taxes.

How is the mortgage secured?

Mortgages are secured through the promissory note.

Is there a redemption period after the sale?

Michigan does not provide a redemption period. However, the state does provide a six-month redemption period for foreclosures and a 30-day redemption period for the sale of abandoned properties. Special statutory protections are given to sellers who finance part of the sale for the buyer.

How is a mortgage lien cancelled?

Mortgage liens are cancelled through a discharge of mortgage.

For how long are judgment liens in effect?

Judgment liens do not expire and do not require renewal.

Can property taxes be paid in installments?

Taxes are assessed on December 1 of each year. Due dates vary by municipality. They can be paid in two installments.

Is this a community property state?

No.

Are title insurance agents regulated?

Agents are regulated by the Division of Insurance. Their rates must be filed with the Division of Insurance but are not regulated.

What is the foreclosure process?

Foreclosure can be carried out by a court or the lender. A judicial foreclosure process must take a minimum of nine months. A non-judicial foreclosure must take a minimum of two months. The sale must be advertised each week for four consecutive weeks. The redemption period is six months.

Who pays closing costs?

Buyers pay closing costs and the title insurance premium. The seller pays the transfer tax and the recording fee.

Who handles consumer complaints?

Complaints can be filed with the following agencies.

1) Office of Insurance Services, 877-999-6442, **http://www.michigan. gov/cis**. 2) Bureau of Commercial Services, 517-241-9267, **http:// www.michigan.gov/cis**.

Section 8.24: MINNESOTA

Land titles are checked how far back into the past?

Titles are researched 40 years into the past or back to their original patent.

Who can perform a real estate closing?

Closings are conducted by attorneys, real estate brokers, real estate sales people, real estate closing agents, lenders, and title companies.

Who can prepare real estate closing documents?

The closing documents can be prepared by anyone.

How can a title be conveyed?

Title is conveyed through warranty deed, guardian's deed, limited warranty deed, quitclaim deed, conservator's deed, trustee's deed, personal representative's deed, or a mortgage or contract in lieu of a deed. Title can be transferred through each of the common law conveyances. They are joint tenancy, tenancy in common and tenancy by the entirety. Titles cannot be held as community property. Married people may hold titles as sole and separate property without consent of spouses. Spousal rights are not assumed.

What are the documentary or transfer taxes and fees?

The transfer taxes vary from one municipality to another. Recording is performed by two county offices. The registrar of titles creates a certificate. The county recorder records said certificate. All fees are determined by these two offices.

Are closing costs open to negotiation?

Closing costs are not negotiable. The custom is a 50-50 split.

What are the mortgage taxes?

Minnesota does not levy mortgage taxes.

How is the mortgage secured?

Mortgages are secured through a promissory note or through a contract for mortgage.

Is there a redemption period after the sale?

Non-foreclosure sales do not have a redemption period. All sales are final.

How is a mortgage lien cancelled?

Mortgage liens are cancelled through a satisfaction of mortgage, partial release of mortgage, or a Uniform Conveying Form Numbers 50-M, 51-M, 51½-M and 131-M.

For how long are judgment liens in effect?

Judgment liens are effective for 10 years. They can be renewed indefinitely.

Can property taxes be paid in installments?

Taxes are levied and assessed in January and are due one year later. They can be paid in two installments due on May 15 and October 15.

Is this a community property state?

No.

Are title insurance agents regulated?

Agents are regulated by the Department of Commerce. Rates must be registered with the Department of Commerce. If the rates are deemed excessive, the agent must provide supportive statistical data.

What is the foreclosure process?

The foreclosure process is usually carried out by the lender without the permission or oversight of a court. The process must take a minimum of 10 weeks. Foreclosures have a redemption period of six months or one year, varying by municipality. If the foreclosure is voluntary, the redemption period is two months. If the property was abandoned the sale redemption period is five weeks.

Who pays closing costs?

The custom is a 50-50 split.

Who handles consumer complaints?

1) Division of Financial Examinations, 651-296-2135, **http://www.state.mn.us/portal/mn/jsp/content.do?programid=536 891197&id=-536882079&agency=Commerce**.

Section 8.25: MISSISSIPPI

Land Titles are checked how far back into the past?

Titles are researched 31 years plus an additional 10 years to cover adverse possession claims. If the titleholder is a minor, the title is researched back 29 years plus 10 years for adverse possession claims. If the minor is married, the title is researched for the standard length of time.

Who can perform a real estate closing?

Closings are conducted by attorneys and lender.

Who can prepare real estate closing documents?

The closing documents are prepared by an attorney or a party involved in the transaction.

How can a title be conveyed?

Title can be conveyed through warranty deed, special warranty deed, quitclaim deed, bargain-and-sale deed or leasehold assignment. Title can be transferred through each of the common law conveyances. They are joint tenancy, tenancy in common, and tenancy by the entirety. Titles cannot be held as community property. Married people may hold titles as sole and separate property without consent of spouses. Spousal rights are not assumed.

What are the documentary or transfer taxes and fees?

Mississippi does not levy transfer taxes. The recording fee is $7 plus $1 for each document attached to the deed. Fifty cents is charged for each related document that must be changed to reflect the new deed.

Are closing costs open to negotiation?

Traditionally buyers and sellers negotiate splitting closing costs, transfer and recording fees, and title insurance premiums when the purchase agreement is created.

What are the mortgage taxes?

Mississippi does not levy mortgage taxes.

How is the mortgage secured?

Mortgages are secured through a deed of trust.

Is there a redemption period after the sale?

Mississippi does not have a post-sale redemption period. All sales are final. Special statutory protections are given to sellers who finance part of the sale for the buyer.

How is a mortgage lien cancelled?

Mortgage liens are cancelled with an authority to cancel, a release, or a partial release. Trustees can cancel a lien by making a marginal notation on the deed.

For how long are judgment liens in effect?

Judgment liens are effective for seven years. After seven years they must be renewed.

Can property taxes be paid in installments?

Taxes are levied and assessed on February 1 and must be paid by the following February 1. Taxes that are in arrears are assessed a 1 percent per month penalty. However, taxes can be paid in three installments. One half is due by February 1. One fourth is due by May 1 and one fourth is due by July 1.

Is this a community property state?

No.

Are title insurance agents regulated?

Agents must be licensed by the Insurance Department, but their fees are not recorded or regulated.

What is the foreclosure process?

The foreclosure process is usually carried out by the lender without the permission or oversight of a court. The process must take a minimum of four months. If the foreclosure is carried out by a court, it must take a minimum of one month. Foreclosures do not have a redemption period.

Who pays closing costs?

Each transaction is different as the tradition is for buyers and sellers to negotiate the fees.

Who handles consumer complaints?

1) Department of Consumer Financing, 601-359-1031, **www.dbcf. state.ms.us**. 2) Mississippi Real Estate Commission, 601-932-9191, **www.mrec.state.ms.us**. 3) Department of Insurance, 800-562-2957, **www.doi.state.ms.us**.

Section 8.26: MISSOURI

Land Titles are checked how far back into the past?

Titles are researched 45 years into the past.

Who can perform a real estate closing?

Closings are conducted by closing companies, title insurance companies, attorneys and real estate agents.

Who can prepare real estate closing documents?

Closing documents can be prepared by attorneys or parties associated with the transaction.

How can a title be conveyed?

Title is conveyed through warranty deed. Title can be transferred through each of the common law conveyances. They are joint tenancy, tenancy in common, and tenancy by the entirety. Titles cannot be held as community property. Married people may hold titles as sole and separate property without consent of spouses. Spousal rights are not assumed.

What are the documentary or transfer taxes and fees?

Missouri does not levy transfer taxes. The recording fees are $9 for the first page and $3 for each additional page.

Are closing costs open to negotiation?

The tradition is to split closing costs.

What are the mortgage taxes?

Missouri does not levy mortgage taxes.

How is the mortgage secured?

Mortgages are secured through a deed of trust that allows private power of sale.

Is there a redemption period after the sale?

Missouri allows a one-year post-sale redemption period.

How is a mortgage lien cancelled?

Mortgage liens are cancelled through release deed.

For how long are judgment liens in effect?

Judgment liens are effective for three years and must be renewed by a scire-facias-writ of revival.

Can property taxes be paid in installments?

Taxes are levied and assessed on January 1 and must be paid by November 1. They cannot be paid in installments.

Is this a community property state?

No.

Are title insurance agents regulated?

Agents and their rates are regulated by statute Mo. Ann. Stat. § 381-011 et seq. (Vernon 1991).

What is the foreclosure process?

The foreclosure process is usually carried out by the lender without the permission or oversight of a court. The process must take a minimum of 21 days. Foreclosures have a redemption period of one year.

Who pays closing costs?

The tradition is to split closing costs.

Who handles consumer complaints?

1) Division of Finance, 573-751-3242, **www.ecodev.state. mo.us/finance**. 2) Department of Insurance, 573-751-2640, **www.insurance.state.mo.us**. 3) Real Estate Commission, 573-751-4352, **www.ecodev.state.mo.us/pr/restate/**.

Section 8.27: MONTANA

Land titles are checked how far back into the past?

Titles are researched back to their original patent.

Who can perform a real estate closing?

Closings are conducted by title companies, attorneys, and lenders.

Who can prepare real estate closing documents?

The closing documents are prepared by an attorney.

How can a title be conveyed?

Titles are conveyed through warranty deed or quit claim deed. Title can be transferred through each of the common law conveyances. They are joint tenancy, tenancy in common, and tenancy by the entirety. Titles cannot be held as community property. Married people may hold titles as sole and separate property without consent of spouses. Spousal rights are not assumed. Montana allows adverse possession with statute Mont. Code Ann. § 70-19-401 through 70-19-421 (1995), after a minimum of five years of possession. Possession is contingent on the payment of property taxes for the real estate taken.

What are the documentary or transfer taxes and fees?

Montana does not charge transfer taxes. The recording fee is $6 per page.

Are closing costs open to negotiation?

The precedent is a 50-50 split.

What are the mortgage taxes?

Montana does not levy mortgage taxes.

How is the mortgage secured?

Mortgages are secured through a deed of sale or sale contract.

Is there a redemption period after the sale?

Standard sales do not have a redemption period. All sales are final. Special protections are given to sellers who finance part of the sale for the buyer under Mont. Code Ann. §§ 71-1-232 and 71-3-114 (1995).

How is a mortgage lien cancelled?

Mortgage liens are cancelled through a satisfaction of mortgage or a reconveyance for trust indenture.

For how long are judgment liens in effect?

Six years, after which they must be renewed by a court pleading.

Can property taxes be paid in installments?

Taxes are levied and assessed on November 30 and must be paid by the following November 30. They can be paid in two installments, due on November 30 and May 31 of the following year. Interest is not charged on these installment payments.

Is this a community property state?

No.

Are title insurance agents regulated?

Agents and their fees are regulated by the Montana Insurance Department.

What is the foreclosure process?

The foreclosure process is usually carried out by the lender, without the permission or oversight of a court. The process must take a minimum of 120 days. Foreclosures have a redemption period of one year.

Who pays closing costs?

The precedent is a 50-50 split.

Who handles consumer complaints?

Complaints can be filed with the following agencies.

1) Department of Commerce, 406-444-2091, **http://sao.mt.gov/**.
2) Department of Insurance, 406-444-2040, **www.state.mt.us/sao**.

Section 8.28: NEBRASKA

Land Titles are checked how far back into the past?

Titles are researched back to their patents.

Who can perform a real estate closing?

Closings can be performed by mortgage brokers, title agents, real estate agents, and attorneys.

Who can prepare real estate closing documents?

The closing documents can be prepared by a closing agent or an attorney.

How can a title be conveyed?

Title is conveyed through warranty deed. Title can be transferred through each of the common law conveyances. They are joint tenancy,

tenancy in common, and tenancy by the entirety. Titles cannot be held as community property. Married people may hold titles as sole and separate property without consent of spouses. Spousal rights are not assumed. Nebraska allows adverse possession after actual, active, continuous, exclusive and notorious possession for a full 10 years.

What are the documentary or transfer taxes and fees?

The transfer taxes are $1.75 for each $1,000. The recording fee is $5 per page and $.50 per lot.

Are closing costs open to negotiation?

The precedent is for buyers and sellers to split closing costs.

What are the mortgage taxes?

Nebraska does not levy mortgage taxes.

How is the mortgage secured?

Mortgages are secured through a deed of trust.

Is there a redemption period after the sale?

Nebraska does not provide a redemption period after the sale. All sales are final. However, judicial foreclosures have a redemption period that ends after the confirmation of the sale. Non-judicial foreclosures have a redemption period that ends after the trustees' deed is recorded. Special statutory rights are given to sellers who finance part of the purchase price for the buyer.

How is a mortgage lien cancelled?

Mortgages liens are cancelled through a release. A deed of reconveyance is used to cancel a deed of trust. Nebraska does not recognize vendor's liens.

For how long are judgment liens in effect?

Judgment liens are effective for five years. Before the end of the five-year period, the creditor must sue the debtor again to renew the lien. If the creditor does not file a new suit before the termination of the previous lien, the lien is void.

Can property taxes be paid in installments?

Taxes are levied and assessed on January 1 and can be paid in two installments, due before April 1 and September 1st. Interest is charged on delinquent taxes only at the rate of 14 percent.

Is this a community property state?

No.

Are title insurance agents regulated?

Agents and their rates are regulated by the Nebraska Department of Insurance.

What is the foreclosure process?

The foreclosure process is usually carried out through a court order. However, a lender can conduct a foreclosure. Judicial foreclosures have a redemption period that ends after the confirmation of the sale. Non-judicial foreclosures have a redemption period that ends after the trustees' deed is recorded. The judicial foreclosure process must take a minimum of either six or eighteen months. The minimum time depends on the type of foreclosure. Non-judicial foreclosures backed by a deed of trust must take a minimum of 90 days.

Who pays closing costs?

The precedent is for buyers and sellers to split closing costs.

Who handles consumer complaints?

Complaints can be filed with the following agencies.

1) Department of Banking and Finance, 402-471-2171, **www.ndbf.org**. 2) Department of Insurance, 402-471-2201, **www.nol.org/home/ndoi**. 3) Real Estate Commission, 402-471-2004, **www.nrec.state.ne.us**.

Section 8.29: NEVADA

Land titles are checked how far back into the past?

Titles are researched back to the last title insurance policy or back to their patent, whichever is applicable.

Who can perform a real estate closing?

Closings can be performed by an escrow officer.

Who can prepare real estate closing documents?

They must be prepared by an attorney licensed by the Nevada bar.

How can a title be conveyed?

Title is conveyed through grant deed, bargain-and-sale deed, or quit claim deed. Title can be transferred through each of the common law conveyances. They are joint tenancy, tenancy in common, and tenancy by the entirety. Titles can be held as community property. Married people may hold titles as sole and separate property, but only with consent of spouses. Spousal rights are assumed. Nevada allows adverse possession after five years of open, notorious possession of the property. However, the party taking possession must pay the property taxes for at least five years into the past before taking title.

What are the documentary or transfer taxes and fees?

Transfer tax is $.75 for each $500 of the sale price. Recording fee is $7 for the first page and $1 for each additional page.

Are closing costs open to negotiation?

The precedent is for buyers and sellers to split closing costs 50-50. The buyer also pays the lender's title insurance policy premium. The seller pays the buyer's title insurance policy premium.

What are the mortgage taxes?

Nevada does not levy mortgage taxes.

How is the mortgage secured?

Mortgages are secured through a deed of trust.

Is there a redemption period after the sale?

No. All sales are final.

How is a mortgage lien cancelled?

They are cancelled through a full or partial reconveyance.

For how long are judgment liens in effect?

Judgment liens are effective for six years. They may be renewed for an additional six years.

Can property taxes be paid in installments?

Taxes are levied and assessed annually by each individual county. They are due by the first Monday in August. Taxes can be paid in quarterly installments due before the first Monday in August, October, January, and March. Delinquent payments are charged 4 percent interest.

Is this a community property state?

Yes.

Are title insurance agents regulated?

Agents are regulated by the Commissioner of Insurance. However, their rates must be filed with the Commissioner of Insurance but are not regulated.

What is the foreclosure process?

The foreclosure process is usually carried out by the lender without the permission or oversight of a court. However, foreclosure can be through court order. The process must take a minimum of 180 days. Foreclosures do not have a redemption period. The foreclosure procedure is complex. The creditor must mail a notice to the debtor within 10 days of initiating foreclosure proceedings. The debtor is then given a 31-day reinstatement period. After the reinstatement period, the creditor may begin advertising the foreclosure. The announcement must be made at least once per week for three weeks.

Who pays closing costs?

The precedent is for buyer and sellers to split closing costs.

Who handles consumer complaints?

1) Department of Business and Industry, 775-684-1830, **www.fid.state.nv.us**. 2) Department of Business and Industry, Division of Insurance, 800-992-0900, **www.doi.state.nv.us**. 3) Real Estate Division, 775-687-4280, **www.red.state.nv.us/**.

Section 8.30: NEW HAMPSHIRE

Land Titles are checked how far back into the past?

Titles are researched 35 years into the past or to the last recorded warranty deed.

Who can perform a real estate closing?

Closings are performed by attorneys and title insurance companies.

Who can prepare real estate closing documents?

The closing documents can be prepared by anyone.

How can a title be conveyed?

Title is conveyed through warranty deed, foreclosure deed, or quit claim deed. Title can be transferred through each of the common law conveyances. They are joint tenancy, tenancy in common, and tenancy by the entirety. Titles cannot be held as community property. Married people may hold titles as sole and separate property without consent of spouses. Spousal rights are not assumed. New Hampshire allows adverse possession after 20 years of open, continuous, exclusive, and notorious possession.

What are the documentary or transfer taxes and fees?

Transfer tax is $.75 for each $100 of the sale price. Recording fee is $10 for the first page and $4 for each subsequent page.

Are closing costs open to negotiation?

Closing fees are negotiable. The custom is a 50-50 split.

What are the mortgage taxes?

New Hampshire does not levy mortgage taxes.

How is the mortgage secured?

Mortgages are secured through a promissory note.

Is there a redemption period after the sale?

New Hampshire does not provide a post-sale redemption period. All sales are final but foreclosures have a one-year redemption period. The state provides a one-year builder's warranty period.

How is a mortgage lien cancelled?

Mortgage liens are cancelled through a discharge.

For how long are judgment liens in effect?

Judgment liens are effective for 20 years. They must be renewed for an additional 20 years.

Can property taxes be paid in installments?

Taxes are levied and assessed annually and must be paid either before July 1 or December 1. They are due by the first Monday in August. Taxes can be paid in two installments, due before July 1 and December 1. Delinquent payments are charged 12 percent interest.

Is this a community property state?

No.

Are title insurance agents regulated?

Agents and their fees are regulated by the State Insurance Department.

What is the foreclosure process?

The foreclosure process is usually carried out by the lender without the permission or oversight of a court. However, foreclosure can be done through court order. The process must take a minimum of 26 days. Foreclosures have a one-year redemption period.

Who pays closing costs?

The custom is a 50-50 split.

Who handles consumer complaints?

Complaints can be filed with the following agencies.

1) Banking Department, 603-271-3561, **www.webster.state. nh.us/banking**. 2) Department of Insurance, 800-852-3416, **www.state.nh.us/insurance**. 3) Real Estate Commission, 603-271-2701, **www.state.nh.us/nhrec**.

Section 8.31: NEW JERSEY

Land titles are checked how far back into the past?

Titles are researched back to the most recent title insurance policy or 60 years into the past, whichever is applicable.

Who can perform a real estate closing?

Closings can be performed by attorneys and title insurance companies in southern New Jersey. The buyer's attorney conducts the closing in northern New Jersey.

Who can prepare real estate closing documents?

The are prepared by any party involved in the transaction.

How can a title be conveyed?

Title is conveyed through a bargain-and-sale deed. Title can be transferred through each of the common law conveyances. They are joint tenancy, tenancy in common, and tenancy by the entirety. Titles cannot be held as community property. Married people may hold titles as sole and separate property without the consent of spouses. Spousal rights are not assumed. New Jersey allows adverse possession after 20 to 60 years of open, notorious, exclusive, continuous, and hostile possession. Adverse possession can be made against government land.

What are the documentary or transfer taxes and fees?

Transfer taxes are $1.75 for each $500 of the gross sale price. Recording fee is $18 for the first page and $2 for each extra page.

Are closing costs open to negotiation?

The precedent is for the buyer to pay all of the closing fees.

What are the mortgage taxes?

New Jersey does not levy mortgage taxes.

How is the mortgage secured?

Mortgages are secured through a promissory note most commonly. They can be secured through a deed of trust.

Is there a redemption period after the sale?

They allow a 10-day redemption period that can be extended by a court if there is reason. State statues allow for a builder's warranty. Refer to N.J. Stat. Ann., § 46:3B-1 et seq. (West 1977).

How is a mortgage lien cancelled?

Mortgage liens are cancelled through a satisfaction endorsed on the mortgage. Mortgages are cancelled through a discharge of mortgage by the lender.

For how long are judgment liens in effect?

Judgment liens are effective for 20 years. They can be renewed for an additional 20 years.

Can property taxes be paid in installments?

They are assessed and levied annually but paid quarterly. The first quarter's bill is estimated based on the previous year's bill. Payment is due by the end of the second month of each quarter. Delinquent taxes are charged interest in the amount of 8 percent. Taxes in amounts more than $1,500 are charged 18 percent interest.

Is this a community property state?

New Jersey is not a community property state.

Are title insurance agents regulated?

They are regulated by the state and must successfully complete a state-run educational program and pass a state examination.

What is the foreclosure process?

Foreclosure is conducted through court order only. The minimum time required to process a foreclosure depends on the court's case load. Typically it is 12 to 18 months. There is a 10-day redemption period after the sale unless ordered otherwise by a court.

Who pays closing costs?

The precedent is for the buyer to pay all of the closing fees.

Who handles consumer complaints?

1) Department of Banking and Insurance, Division of Banking, 609-984-2777, **www.state.nj.us/dobi**. 2) Department of Banking and Insurance, Division of Insurance, 800-446-7467, **www.state.nj.us/dobi**. 3) Department of Banking and Insurance, Division of Real Estate, 609-292-8300, **www.state.nj.us/dobi.remnu.htm**.

Section 8.32: NEW MEXICO

Land Titles are checked how far back into the past?

Titles are researched 30 years into the past.

Who can perform a real estate closing?

Closings are conducted by escrow officers.

Who can prepare real estate closing documents?

Closing documents are prepared by attorneys.

How can a title be conveyed?

Title is conveyed through warranty deed. Title can be transferred through each of the common law conveyances. They are joint tenancy, tenancy in common, and tenancy by the entirety. Titles can be held as community property. Married people may hold titles as sole and separate property but only with consent of spouses. Spousal rights are assumed. New Mexico recognizes adverse possession after 10 years of continuous possession.

What are the documentary or transfer taxes and fees?

New Mexico does not levy transfer taxes. The recording fees are $7 for the first page and $2 for each additional page.

Are closing costs open to negotiation?

The precedent is for closing costs to be divided equally.

What are the mortgage taxes?

New Mexico does not levy mortgage taxes.

How is the mortgage secured?

Mortgages are secured through a deed of trust.

Is there a redemption period after the sale?

They provide a nine-month redemption period. This period can be reduced by one month in the purchase contract but cannot be completely waived. Special protections are given to sellers who finance part of the sale for the buyer under state statute.

How is a mortgage lien cancelled?

Mortgage liens are cancelled through release of mortgage.

For how long are judgment liens in effect?

Judgment liens are effective for 14 years and cannot be renewed.

Can property taxes be paid in installments?

Taxes are levied by mail on November 1 and are due 30 days after the postmark. There is a 10-day grace period. The tax can be paid in two installments that are due on December 10 and May 10. An interest rate of 1 percent is applied to installments. However, no more than 5 percent interest will be charged.

Is this a community property state?

New Mexico is a community property state.

Are title insurance agents regulated?

Agents and their rates are regulated by the New Mexico Department of Insurance.

What is the foreclosure process?

Foreclosure is conducted through court order only. The minimum time required to process a foreclosure is nine months. There is a nine-month redemption period after the sale unless ordered otherwise by a court.

Who pays closing costs?

The precedent is for closing costs to be divided equally.

Who handles consumer complaints?

1)   Regulation   and   Licensing   Department,   505-827-4601,

www.nmprc.state.nm.us. 2) Real Estate Commission, 800-801-7505, www.state.nm.us/nmrec.

Section 8.33: NEW YORK

Land Titles are checked how far back into the past?

Titles are researched 40 years into the past.

Who can perform a real estate closing?

Closings can be performed by attorneys.

Who can prepare real estate closing documents?

Closing documents are prepared by an attorney.

How can a title be conveyed?

Title is conveyed through bargain-and-sale deed. Title can be transferred through each of the common law conveyances. They are joint tenancy, tenancy in common, and tenancy by the entirety. Titles can be held as community property. Married people may hold titles as sole and separate property but only with consent of spouses. Spousal rights are assumed. New York recognizes adverse possession after 10 years.

What are the documentary or transfer taxes and fees?

The transfer taxes are in the form of a capital gains tax. It is $4 per $1,000 gained. The recording fee is $15 for the first page and $5 for each additional page.

Are closing costs open to negotiation?

The precedent is for the buyer to pay all of the closing fees including the title insurance premiums.

What are the mortgage taxes?

The mortgage taxes are .75 percent of the amount owed for upstate residents and 1 percent of what is owed downstate and 2 percent for New York City residents.

How is the mortgage secured?

Mortgages are secured through the promissory note.

Is there a redemption period after the sale?

No. All sales are final.

How is a mortgage lien cancelled?

Mortgage liens are cancelled through a satisfaction of mortgage.

For how long are judgment liens in effect?

Judgment liens are effective for 10 years. They must be renewed for an additional 10 years.

Can property taxes be paid in installments?

Taxes are levied and assessed annually and are due on January 1 or July 1. Taxes can be paid in two installments due before January 1 and July 1. Delinquent payments are charged interest, but the amount varies by municipality.

Is this a community property state?

Yes.

Are title insurance agents regulated?

Agents are not regulated, but title insurance rates are strictly regulated.

What is the foreclosure process?

The foreclosure process is usually carried out by the lender without the permission or oversight of a court. However, foreclosure can be through court order. The process must take a minimum of 180 days. Foreclosures do not have a redemption period.

Who pays closing costs?

The precedent is for the buyer to pay all of the closing fees including the title insurance premiums.

Who handles consumer complaints?

1) Banking Department, 518-474-6600, **www.ins.state.ny.us**. 2) Department of State, Division of Licensing Services, 518-474-4429, **www.dos.state.ny.us/lcns/licensing.html**.

Section 8.34: NORTH CAROLINA

Land Titles are checked how far back into the past?

Titles are researched 30 to 40 years into the past.

Who can perform a real estate closing?

Closings are performed by an attorney.

Who can prepare real estate closing documents?

Closing documents can be prepared by attorneys and their staff.

How can a title be conveyed?

Titles are conveyed through warranty deed. Title can be transferred through each of the common law conveyances. They are joint tenancy, tenancy in common, and tenancy by the entirety. Titles can be held as community property. Married people may hold titles as sole and separate property without consent of spouses. Spousal rights are not assumed. North Carolina recognizes adverse possession after 20 years of physical possession.

What are the documentary or transfer taxes and fees?

The transfer tax is $1 for each $500 of the sale price. The recording fee is $6 for the first page and $2 for each additional page.

Are closing costs open to negotiation?

Closing fees are negotiable.

What are the mortgage taxes?

North Carolina does not levy mortgage taxes.

How is the mortgage secured?

Mortgages are secured through a deed of trust.

Is there a redemption period after the sale?

North Carolina allows a 10-day redemption period after the sale.

How is a mortgage lien cancelled?

Mortgage liens are cancelled by recording the original lien documents with a satisfaction entry or by recording a release deed.

For how long are judgment liens in effect?

Judgment liens are effective for 10 years. The may be renewed for an additional 10 years.

Can property taxes be paid in installments?

Taxes are levied and assessed on January 1 and are due by September 1. Taxes cannot be paid in installments. Delinquent payments are not charged interest.

Is this a community property state?

North Carolina is not a community property state.

Are title insurance agents regulated?

Agents must be licensed through the Commissioner of Insurance. Their rates must be filed with the Commissioner of Insurance.

What is the foreclosure process?

The foreclosure process is usually carried out by the lender without the permission or oversight of a court. However, foreclosure can be through court order. The process must take a minimum of 60 days. Foreclosures have a 10-day redemption period.

Who pays closing costs?

Closing fees are negotiable.

Who handles consumer complaints?

1) Commissioner of Banks, 919-733-3016, **www.banking. state.nc.us/**. 2) Department of Insurance, 800-546-5664, **www.ncdoi.com/**. 3) Real Estate Commission, 919-875-3700, **www. ncrec.state.nc.us/**.

Section 8.35: NORTH DAKOTA

Land Titles are checked how far back into the past?

Titles are researched back to their original U.S. patent.

Who can perform a real estate closing?

Closings can be performed by lenders, title companies, attorneys and real estate agents.

Who can prepare real estate closing documents?

Closing documents must be prepared by an attorney.

How can a title be conveyed?

Title is conveyed through warranty deed. Title can be transferred through each of the common law conveyances. They are joint tenancy, tenancy in common, and tenancy by the entirety. Titles can be held as community property. Married people may hold titles as sole and separate property without consent of spouses. Spousal rights are not assumed. North Dakota recognizes adverse possession after either 10 or 20 years of open and notorious physical possession.

What are the documentary or transfer taxes and fees?

North Dakota does not levy a transfer tax. The recording fee is $10 for the first page and $3 for each additional page.

Are closing costs open to negotiation?

The precedent is for the buyer to pay all of the closing fees.

What are the mortgage taxes?

North Dakota does not levy mortgage taxes.

How is the mortgage secured?

Mortgages are secured through the promissory note.

Is there a redemption period after the sale?

There is a six-month redemption period after the sale.

How is a mortgage lien cancelled?

Mortgage liens are cancelled through a satisfaction and release.

For how long are judgment liens in effect?

Judgment liens are effective for 10 years. They must be renewed within 90 days of the expiration of the current lien via an affidavit submitted by the creditor.

Can property taxes be paid in installments?

Taxes are levied and assessed annually and are due semiannually. Taxes can be paid in two installments due on March 15 and October 15. Delinquent payments are not charged interest.

Is this a community property state?

No.

Are title insurance agents regulated?

Agents and their fees are regulated by the North Dakota Insurance Department.

What is the foreclosure process?

Foreclosure is usually conducted through court order. The minimum time required to process a foreclosure is 180 days. There is a six-month redemption period after the sale.

Who pays closing costs?

The precedent is for the buyer to pay all of the closing fees.

Who handles consumer complaints?

1) Department of Financial Institutions, 701-328-9933, **www.state.nd.us/bank**. 2) Department of Insurance, 800-247-0560, **www.state.nd.us/ndins**. 3) Real Estate Commission, 701-328-9749.

Section 8.36: OHIO

Land Titles are checked how far back into the past?

Titles are usually researched back 60 years. This period is not regulated.

Who can perform a real estate closing?

Closings can be conducted by banks, attorneys, and title insurance companies.

Who can prepare real estate closing documents?

They can be prepared by an attorney or by the grantor.

How can a title be conveyed?

Title is conveyed by warranty deed, limited warranty deed, or quit claim deed. Title can be transferred through each of the common law conveyances. They are joint tenancy, tenancy in common, and tenancy by the entirety. Titles can be held as community property. Married people may hold titles as sole and separate property without consent of spouses. Spousal rights are not assumed. Ohio recognizes adverse possession after either 10 or 21 years of open and adverse physical possession.

What are the documentary or transfer taxes and fees?

The transfer tax is either $1 or $4 for each $1,000 of the sale price. The recording fee is $14 for the first two pages and $4 for each additional page.

Are closing costs open to negotiation?

Closing costs are negotiable.

What are the mortgage taxes?

Ohio does not levy mortgage taxes.

How is the mortgage secured?

Mortgages are secured through the promissory note.

Is there a redemption period after the sale?

No.

How is a mortgage lien cancelled?

Mortgage liens are cancelled through a release of mortgage.

For how long are judgment liens in effect?

Judgment liens are effective for five years. They can be renewed.

Can property taxes be paid in installments?

Taxes are levied and assessed semiannually are due on June 20 and December 20. Taxes can be paid in two installments. Delinquent payments are charged 5 percent interest. Delinquent payments can be broken into five installments.

Is this a community property state?

No.

Are title insurance agents regulated?

They are regulated by the Department of Insurance.

What is the foreclosure process?

It is conducted through court order only. Minimum time required to process a foreclosure is 5 months. There is no redemption period after the sale unless ordered otherwise by a court.

Who pays closing costs?

Closing costs are negotiable.

Who handles consumer complaints?

1) Division of Financial Institutions, 614-728-8400, **www.scom.state. oh.us/ODOC/dfi/**. 2) Department of Insurance, 614-644-2658, **www. ins.state.oh.us/**. 3) Department of Commerce, Division of Real Estate, 614-466-4100, **www.com.state.oh.us/ODOC/real/**.

Section 8.37: OKLAHOMA

Land titles are checked how far back into the past?

Titles are researched back to sovereignty.

Who can perform a real estate closing?

Closings can be conducted by title insurance companies, independent closing companies, and attorneys.

Who can prepare real estate closing documents?

Closing documents can be prepared by title insurance companies, independent closing companies, and attorneys.

How can a title be conveyed?

Through warranty deed, quitclaim deed, special warranty deed, and court order. Title can be transferred through each of the common law conveyances. They are joint tenancy, tenancy in common, and tenancy by the entirety. Titles can be held as community property. Married people may hold titles as sole and separate property without consent of spouses. Spousal rights are not assumed Oklahoma recognizes adverse possession after 15 years of open and adverse physical possession.

What are the documentary or transfer taxes and fees?

The transfer tax is $.75 for each $500. The recording fee is $8 for the first page and $2 for each additional page.

Are closing costs open to negotiation?

Closing fees are negotiable.

What are the mortgage taxes?

Mortgage taxes are paid by the lender.

How is the mortgage secured?

Mortgages are secured through a promissory note.

Is there a redemption period after the sale?

No.

How is a mortgage lien cancelled?

Mortgage liens are cancelled through a release of mortgage.

For how long are judgment liens in effect?

Judgment liens are effective for five years but can be renewed.

Can property taxes be paid in installments?

Taxes are levied and assessed after January 1 and must be paid before November 1. Taxes can be paid in two installments due before January 1 and March 31. Delinquent payments are not charged interest, but a penalty is imposed.

Is this a community property state?

No.

Are title insurance agents regulated?

Agents are regulated by the Department of Insurance. However, their rates are not regulated.

What is the foreclosure process?

Foreclosure is conducted through court order only. The minimum time required to process a foreclosure is determined by the applicable state statute. There is no redemption period after the sale unless ordered otherwise by a court.

Who pays closing costs?

Closing fees are negotiable.

Who handles consumer complaints?

1) State Banking Department, 405-521-3653, **www.state.ok.us/~osbd**. 2) Insurance Department, 405-521-2828, **www.oid.state.ok.us**. 3) Real Estate Commission, 405-521-3387, **www.state.ok.us/~orec/**.

Section 8.38: OREGON

Land Titles are checked how far back into the past?

Titles are researched back to their U.S. patent.

Who can perform a real estate closing?

Closings are conducted by an escrow agent.

Who can prepare real estate closing documents?

Closing documents are prepared by an escrow agent or by an attorney in complex closings.

How can a title be conveyed?

Title is conveyed through warranty deed or bargain-and-sale deed. Title can be transferred through each of the common law conveyances. They are joint tenancy, tenancy in common, and tenancy by the entirety. Titles can be held as community property. Married people may hold titles as sole and separate property without consent of spouses. Spousal rights are not assumed. Oregon recognizes adverse possession after 10 years of honest belief ownership.

What are the documentary or transfer taxes and fees?

The transfer tax is 1 percent of the sale price. The recording fees vary with each county.

Are closing costs open to negotiation?

The precedent is a 50-50 split.

What are the mortgage taxes?

Oregon does not levy mortgage taxes.

How is the mortgage secured?

Mortgages are secured through deed of trust.

Is there a redemption period after the sale?

Oregon provides a six-month redemption period.

How is a mortgage lien cancelled?

Mortgage liens are cancelled through mortgage-satisfaction, trust-deeds, deeds of reconveyance, and contract-fulfillment deeds.

For how long are judgment liens in effect?

For 10 years and eligible for renewal.

Can property taxes be paid in installments?

Taxes are levied and assessed in October and must be paid before November 15. They transfer into a lien on July 1. Taxes can be paid in three installments due before November 15, February 15, and May 15. Delinquent payments are charged interest of 1-1/3 percent.

Is this a community property state?

No.

Are title insurance agents regulated?

Agents and their fees are regulated by the Insurance Division, Department of Consumer and Business Services

What is the foreclosure process?

The foreclosure process is usually carried out by the lender without the permission or oversight of a court. However, foreclosure can be through court order. The process must take a minimum of 120 days. Oregon provides a six-month redemption period.

Who pays closing costs?

The precedent is a 50-50 split.

Who handles consumer complaints?

1) Insurance Division, 503-947-7980, TYY 503-947-7280, **www.cbs.state.or.us/ins**. 2) Real Estate Agency, 503-378-4170, **www.rea.state.or.us/**.

Section 8.39: PENNSYLVANIA

Land titles are checked how far back into the past?

Titles are researched 60 years into the past.

Who can perform a real estate closing?

Agents of title companies or by attorneys.

Who can prepare real estate closing documents?

They are prepared by agents of title companies or by attorneys.

How can a title be conveyed?

Title is conveyed through special warranty deed or through warranty deed. Titles can be transferred through each of the common law conveyances. They are joint tenancy, tenancy in common, and tenancy by the entirety. Titles can be held as community property. Married people may hold titles as sole and separate property without consent of spouses. Spousal rights are not assumed.

What are the documentary or transfer taxes and fees?

Transfer tax is 1 percent of the appraised value of the real estate. Pittsburgh charges three percent and Philadelphia charges 2-½ percent. The recording fee varies from $15.50 to $50 for the first four pages and from $2 to $4 for all subsequent pages.

Are closing costs open to negotiation?

The precedent is a 50-50 split.

What are the mortgage taxes?

Pennsylvania does not levy mortgage taxes.

How is the mortgage secured?

Mortgages are secured through the promissory note.

Is there a redemption period after the sale?

No.

How is a mortgage lien cancelled?

Through a mortgage satisfaction piece. A partial lien release is conveyed with a release of mortgage.

For how long are judgment liens in effect?

Judgment liens are effective for five years and can only be renewed through court order.

Can property taxes be paid in installments?

Taxes are levied and assessed annually and must be paid by mid-March. They cannot be paid in installments except in Pittsburgh.

Is this a community property state?

Pennsylvania is not a community property state.

Are title insurance agents regulated?

Agents and their fees are regulated by the Insurance Department. Agents must pass a written exam.

What is the foreclosure process?

Foreclosure is usually conducted through court order. The minimum time required to process a foreclosure is six months. There is no redemption period after the sale.

Who pays closing costs?

The precedent is a 50-50 split.

Who handles consumer complaints?

1) Department of Banking, 717-787-1854, TDD 1-800-679-5070, **www.banking.state.pa.us/**. 2) Bureau of Consumer Service, 877-881-6388, **www.insurance.state.pa.us**. 3) Real Estate Commission, 717-783-3658, **www.dos.state.pa.us/bpoa**.

Section 8.40: RHODE ISLAND

Land titles are checked how far back into the past?

Titles are researched 50 years into the past.

Who can perform a real estate closing?

Closings are conducted by title companies and attorneys.

Who can prepare real estate closing documents?

They are prepared by title companies and attorneys.

How can a title be conveyed?

Title is conveyed through warranty deed, quitclaim deed, or bargain-and-sale deed. Title can be transferred through each of the common law conveyances. They are joint tenancy, tenancy in common, and tenancy by the entirety. Titles can be held as community property. Married people may hold titles as sole and separate property without consent of spouses. Spousal rights are not assumed. Rhode Island recognizes adverse possession after 10 years of adverse and notorious ownership.

What are the documentary or transfer taxes and fees?

Transfer tax is $2.80 for each $1,000 of the sale price. Recording fee is $25.

Are closing costs open to negotiation?

The precedent is a 50-50 split.

What are the mortgage taxes?

Rhode Island does not levy mortgage taxes.

How is the mortgage secured?

Mortgages are secured through a deed of trust.

Is there a redemption period after the sale?

No. However, foreclosures have a three-year redemption period.

How is a mortgage lien cancelled?

By recording the original documents with "Paid and Fully Satisfied" written across the front. The creditor must date and sign the document with at least one witness.

For how long are judgment liens in effect?

Judgment liens are effective for varying times depending on the type of lien. Refer to the state statutes.

Can property taxes be paid in installments?

Taxes are levied on December 31. The due dates vary. Taxes can be paid in four installments with due dates varying by city.

Is this a community property state?

Rhode Island is not a community property state.

Are title insurance agents regulated?

Agents and their rates are regulated by the Department of Business.

What is the foreclosure process?

The foreclosure process is usually carried out by the lender without the permission or oversight of a court. However, foreclosure can be through court order. The process must take a minimum of 42 days. Rhode Island does not provide a redemption period.

Who pays closing costs?

The precedent is a 50-50 split.

Who handles consumer complaints?

1) Department of Business Regulation, 401-222-2495, TDD 401-222-2999, **www.dbr.state.ri.us**. 2) Commercial Licensing and Regulation Division, Real Estate, 401-222-2255, TDD 401-222-2999, **www.dbr.state.ri.us/real_estate.html**.

Section 8.41: SOUTH CAROLINA

Land titles are checked how far back into the past?

Titles are researched 40 years into the past.

Who can perform a real estate closing?

Closings are conducted by attorneys.

Who can prepare real estate closing documents?

Closing documents are prepared by attorneys.

How can a title be conveyed?

Through a conveyance instrument in the presence of two witnesses. Title can be transferred through each of the common law conveyances (joint tenancy, tenancy in common, and tenancy by the entirety). Titles can be held as community property. Married people may hold titles as sole and separate property without consent of spouses. Spousal rights are not assumed.

What are the documentary or transfer taxes and fees?

Transfer taxes are $1.85 for each $500 of the sale price. Recording fee is $10 for the first four pages and $1 for each additional page.

Are closing costs open to negotiation?

The precedent is for the buyer to pay closing costs.

What are the mortgage taxes?

South Carolina does not levy mortgage taxes.

How is the mortgage secured?

Mortgages are secured through a promissory note.

Is there a redemption period after the sale?

No.

How is a mortgage lien cancelled?

By recording the original documents with "Paid and Fully Satisfied" written across the front. The creditor must date and sign the document with at least one witness.

For how long are judgment liens in effect?

Judgment liens are effective for 10 years.

Can property taxes be paid in installments?

Taxes are levied in arrears once each year and are due by January 15. They cannot be paid in installments.

Is this a community property state?

This is not a community property state.

Are title insurance agents regulated?

Agents and their rates are regulated by the Insurance Department.

What is the foreclosure process?

Foreclosure is usually conducted through court order. The minimum time required to process a foreclosure is four to six months. There is no redemption period after the sale.

Who pays closing costs?

The precedent is for the buyer to pay closing costs.

Who handles consumer complaints?

1) Department of Consumer Affairs, 803-734-9450, **www.state.sc.us**.
2) Department of Insurance, 803-737-6180, **www.state.sc.us/doi/
Consumer.html**. 3) Real Estate Commission, 803-896-4400, **www.
llr.state.sc.us/POL/RealEstateCommission**.

Section 8.42: SOUTH DAKOTA

Land titles are checked how far back into the past?

Titles are researched back to their U. S. patents.

Who can perform a real estate closing?

The title companies, real estate agents, lenders, and attorneys.

Who can prepare real estate closing documents?

Closing documents are prepared by attorneys.

How can a title be conveyed?

Title is conveyed through warranty deed and quit claim deed. Title
can be transferred through each of the common law conveyances.
They are joint tenancy, tenancy in common, and tenancy by the
entirety. Titles can be held as community property. Married people
may hold titles as sole and separate property without consent of
spouses. Spousal rights are not assumed. South Dakota recognizes
adverse possession after 20 years of adverse ownership.

What are the documentary or transfer taxes and fees?

Transfer taxes are $1 for each $1,000. Recording fee is $10 for the first
page and $2 for each additional page.

Are closing costs open to negotiation?

The precedent is a 50-50 split.

What are the mortgage taxes?

South Dakota does not levy mortgage taxes.

How is the mortgage secured?

Mortgages are secured through a promissory note.

Is there a redemption period after the sale?

The redemption period is one year if the purchase was less than 40 acres. The state statutes allow a short-term redemption mortgage of 180 days.

How is a mortgage lien cancelled?

Mortgage liens are cancelled through a satisfaction of mortgage.

For how long are judgment liens in effect?

Judgment liens are effective for 10 years and can be renewed for an additional 10 years.

Can property taxes be paid in installments?

Taxes are levied on January 1 in arrears and are due on the same date. They can be paid in two installments due before May 1 and November 1. Installments are charged interest at 1 percent.

Is this a community property state?

No.

Are title insurance agents regulated?

Agents and their rates are regulated by the South Dakota Insurance Office.

What is the foreclosure process?

Foreclosure is usually conducted through court order. The minimum time required to process a foreclosure is eight months. The redemption period is one year if the purchase was less than 40 acres. The state statutes allow a short-term redemption mortgage of 180 days.

Who pays closing costs?

The precedent is a 50-50 split.

Who handles consumer complaints?

1) Division of Banking, 605-773-3421, **www.state.sd.us/dcr/ bank**. 2) Division of Insurance, 605-773-3563, **www.state. sd.us/insurance**. 3) Real Estate Commission, 605-773-3600, **www.state.sd.us**.

Section 8.43: TENNESSEE

Land titles are checked how far back into the past?

Titles are researched until the examiner is satisfied.

Who can perform a real estate closing?

Closings are conducted by attorneys.

Who can prepare real estate closing documents?

Closing documents are prepared by attorneys.

How can a title be conveyed?

Title is conveyed through warranty deed or quit claim deed. Titles can be transferred through each of the common law conveyances. They are joint tenancy, tenancy in common, and tenancy by the entirety. Titles can be held as community property. Married people may hold titles as sole and separate property without consent of spouses. Spousal rights are not assumed. Tennessee recognizes adverse possession after seven years of adverse ownership.

What are the documentary or transfer taxes and fees?

Transfer tax is $3.70 for each $1,000 on deeds and $1.15 for each $1,000 on deeds of trust. A $1 clerk fee is charged for each document.

Are closing costs open to negotiation?

The precedent is for a 50-50 split.

What are the mortgage taxes?

The mortgage tax is $1.15 per $1,000 and a $1 clerk fee.

How is the mortgage secured?

Mortgages are secured through a deed of trust.

Is there a redemption period after the sale?

No.

How is a mortgage lien cancelled?

Mortgage liens are cancelled through a release deed.

For how long are judgment liens in effect?

Liens expire after 10 years.

Can property taxes be paid in installments?

Taxes are assessed and levied throughout the year but are due on October 1. Counties will arrange installments that are charged 1.5 percent interest.

Is this a community property state?

This is not a community property state.

Are title insurance agents regulated?

Agents are regulated and their fees are recorded by the Insurance Commission.

What is the foreclosure process?

The process is usually carried out by the lender without the permission or oversight of a court. However, foreclosure can be through court order. The process must take a minimum of 21 days. Tennessee does not provide a redemption period.

Who pays closing costs?

The precedent is for a 50-50 split.

Who handles consumer complaints?

1) Division of Consumer Affairs, 615-741-4737, **www.state.tn.us/ consumer**. 2) Department of Commerce and Insurance, 615-741-2241, **www.state.tn.us/commerce**.

Section 8.44: TEXAS

Land titles are checked how far back into the past?

Titles are researched back to sovereignty.

Who can perform a real estate closing?

Closings are conducted by title companies and attorneys.

Who can prepare real estate closing documents?

The closing documents must be prepared by an attorney.

How can a title be conveyed?

Title is conveyed through warranty deed or special warranty deed. Title can be transferred through each of the common law conveyances. They are joint tenancy, tenancy in common, and tenancy by the entirety. Titles can be held as community property. Married people may hold titles as sole and separate property but only with consent of spouses. Spousal rights are assumed Adverse possession is determined by a court.

What are the documentary or transfer taxes and fees?

Texas does not charge transfer taxes. The recording fee is $4 for the first page and $3 for each additional page.

Are closing costs open to negotiation?

The closing fees are negotiable. The custom is a 50-50 split.

What are the mortgage taxes?

Texas does not levy mortgage taxes.

How is the mortgage secured?

Mortgages are secured through a deed of trust.

Is there a redemption period after the sale?

No.

How is a mortgage lien cancelled?

Mortgage liens are cancelled through a release.

For how long are judgment liens in effect?

For 10 years but can be renewed for an additional 10 years.

Can property taxes be paid in installments?

Taxes are assessed and levied by the end of October. They are due by February 1 of the following year. They cannot be paid in installments.

Is this a community property state?

Yes.

Are title insurance agents regulated?

Agents and their fees are regulated by the Department of Insurance.

What is the foreclosure process?

The process is usually carried out by the lender without the permission or oversight of a court. However, foreclosure can be through court order. The process must take a minimum of 21 days. Texas does not provide a redemption period.

Who pays closing costs?

The custom is a 50-50 split.

Who handles consumer complaints?

1) State Finance Commission, 877-276-5554, **www.fc.state.tx.us/**. 2)

Department of Insurance, 800-578-4677, **www.tdi.state.tx.us**. 3) Real Estate Commission, 800-250-8732, **www.tec.state.tx.us**.

Section 8.45: UTAH

Land titles are checked how far back into the past?

Titles are researched 40 years into the past.

Who can perform a real estate closing?

The title companies, lenders, and attorneys.

Who can prepare real estate closing documents?

The closing documents are prepared by a title company.

How can a title be conveyed?

Title is conveyed through a quitclaim deed, special warranty deed, or warranty deed. Title can be transferred through each of the common law conveyances. They are joint tenancy, tenancy in common, and tenancy by the entirety. Titles can be held as community property. Married people may hold titles as sole and separate property without consent of spouses. Spousal rights are not assumed. Utah recognizes adverse possession after seven years with possession and payment of taxes.

What are the documentary or transfer taxes and fees?

Utah does not levy transfer taxes. The recording fee is $10 for the first page and $2 for each additional page.

Are closing costs open to negotiation?

The precedent is a 50-50 split.

What are the mortgage taxes?

Utah does not levy mortgage taxes.

How is the mortgage secured?

Through a deed of trust with power of sale.

Is there a redemption period after the sale?

No.

How is a mortgage lien cancelled?

Mortgage liens are cancelled through a deed of reconveyance.

For how long are judgment liens in effect?

For eight years but can be renewed by a court order.

Can property taxes be paid in installments?

Taxes are levied and assessed by October 1 and are due by November 30 at noon. They cannot be paid in installments.

Is this a community property state?

This is not a community property state.

Are title insurance agents regulated?

Yes, by the Insurance Department, however their fees are not.

What is the foreclosure process?

The process is usually carried out by the lender without the permission or oversight of a court. However, foreclosure can be through court order. The process must take a minimum of 120 days. Utah does not provide a redemption period.

Who pays closing costs?

The precedent is a 50-50 split.

Who handles consumer complaints?

1) Department of Commerce, 801-530-4849, **www.commerce.utah. gov/cor/index.html**. 2) Insurance Department, 801-538-3805, TDD 801-538-3826, **www.insurance.state.ut.us**.

Section 8.46: VERMONT

Land titles are checked how far back into the past?

Titles are researched 40 years into the past.

Who can perform a real estate closing?

Closings are conducted by attorneys.

Who can prepare real estate closing documents?

Closing documents are prepared by lenders and attorneys.

How can a title be conveyed?

By warranty deed, executor's deed, limited warranty deed, or quit claim deed. Title can be transferred through each of the common law conveyances (joint tenancy, tenancy in common, and tenancy by the entirety). Titles can be held as community property. Married people may hold titles as sole and separate property without consent of spouses. Spousal rights are not assumed. Vermont recognizes adverse possession after 15 years.

What are the documentary or transfer taxes and fees?

The transfer tax is 1.25 percent of the appraised value. If the property will be a primary residence, the tax is .5 percent of the appraised value.

Are closing costs open to negotiation?

The precedent is a 50-50 split.

What are the mortgage taxes?

Vermont does not levy mortgage taxes.

How is the mortgage secured?

Mortgages are secured through a promissory note. However, very large transactions are secured through deeds of trust.

Is there a redemption period after the sale?

Vermont allows a one-year redemption period that can be shortened by court order.

How is a mortgage lien cancelled?

They are discharged through an entry on the margin of the record.

For how long are judgment liens in effect?

They are effective for eight years. After expiration they must be renewed by the creditor in a court proceeding.

Can property taxes be paid in installments?

Taxes are levied and assessed according to the statutes of each town.

Is this a community property state?

No.

Are title insurance agents regulated?

Agents and their rates are regulated by the Vermont Department of Banking, Insurance and Securities.

What is the foreclosure process?

Foreclosure is conducted through court order only. The minimum time required to process a foreclosure is determined by the court. There is no redemption period after the sale unless ordered otherwise by a court.

Who pays closing costs?

The precedent is a 50-50 split.

Who handles consumer complaints?

1) Department of Banking, Insurance, Securities and Health Care Administration, 802-828-3307, **www.bishca.state.vt.us/**. 2) Real Estate Commission, 802-828-2363, **www.vtprofessionals.org/ opr1/real_estate/**.

Section 8.47: VIRGINIA

Land titles are checked how far back into the past?

Titles are researched 60 years into the past.

Who can perform a real estate closing?

Attorneys, title companies, and escrow agents.

Who can prepare real estate closing documents?

The closing documents are prepared by attorneys.

How can a title be conveyed?

Title is conveyed through general warranty deed or special warranty deed. Title can be transferred through each of the common law conveyances. They are joint tenancy, tenancy in common, and tenancy by the entirety. Titles can be held as community property. Married people may hold titles as sole and separate property without consent of spouses. Spousal rights are not assumed. Virginia recognizes adverse possession after 15 years of open, notorious, and continuous possession.

What are the documentary or transfer taxes and fees?

Transfer tax is $1 for each $1,000 of the sale price. Recording fee is $14 for the first four pages and $1 for each additional page.

Are closing costs open to negotiation?

The precedent is for the buyer to pay all closing costs.

What are the mortgage taxes?

Virginia does not levy mortgage taxes.

How is the mortgage secured?

Mortgages are secured through a deed of trust.

Is there a redemption period after the sale?

No.

How is a mortgage lien cancelled?

Through a deed release and a certificate of satisfaction.

For how long are judgment liens in effect?

For 20 years and are eligible for renewal.

Can property taxes be paid in installments?

Taxes are levied and assessed by jurisdiction with each having its own due dates and regulations.

Is this a community property state?

No.

Are title insurance agents regulated?

Agents are licensed through the Department of Insurance and their fees are regulated by the same agency.

What is the foreclosure process?

The process is usually carried out by the lender without the permission or oversight of a court. However, foreclosure can be through court order. The process must take a minimum of 30 days. Virginia does not provide a redemption period.

Who pays closing costs?

The precedent is for the buyer to pay all of closing costs.

Who handles consumer complaints?

1) State Corporation Commission, 804-371-9705, TDD 804-371-9206, **www.state.va.us/scc/division/banking**. 2) Department of Professional and Occupational Regulation, 804-367-8500, TDD 804-367-9753, **www.state.va.us/dpor/indexie.html**.

Section 8.48: WASHINGTON

Land titles are checked how far back into the past?

Back to the last title insurance policy or the original U. S. patent.

Who can perform a real estate closing?

Closings are conducted by attorneys.

Who can prepare real estate closing documents?

Closing documents are prepared by attorneys.

How can a title be conveyed?

Title is conveyed through warranty deed. Title can be transferred through each of the common law conveyances. They are joint tenancy, tenancy in common, and tenancy by the entirety. Titles can be held as community property. Married people may hold titles as sole and separate property but only with consent of spouses. Spousal rights are assumed. Washington recognizes adverse possession after 10 years of open, notorious, and continuous possession.

What are the documentary or transfer taxes and fees?

Washington charges an excise tax that is 1.78 percent of the sale price. The recording fee is $2 for the first page and $1 for each additional page.

Are closing costs open to negotiation?

The precedent is a 50-50 split.

What are the mortgage taxes?

Washington does not levy mortgage taxes.

How is the mortgage secured?

Mortgages are secured through a deed of trust.

Is there a redemption period after the sale?

There is a 120-day redemption period for internal revenue sales only. All other sales do not have a redemption period.

How is a mortgage lien cancelled?

Through a reconveyance or the deed of trust.

For how long are judgment liens in effect?

Judgment liens are effective for 10 years but can be renewed.

Can property taxes be paid in installments?

Taxes are levied annually and can be paid in two installments that are due by April 30 and October 31. The installments include 10 percent interest.

Is this a community property state?

Yes.

Are title insurance agents regulated?

Agents and their rates are regulated by the Insurance Commissioner.

What is the foreclosure process?

Foreclosure is usually conducted through court order. The minimum time required to process a foreclosure is 180 days. There is a 120-day redemption period for internal revenue sales only. All other sales do not have a redemption period.

Who pays closing costs?

The precedent is a 50-50 split.

Who handles consumer complaints?

1) Department of Financial Institutions, 800-372-8303, **www.dfi. wa.gov/**. 2) Office of the Commissioner of Insurance, 360-753-3613, TDD 360-407-0409, **www.insurance.wa.gov**.

Section 8.49: WEST VIRGINIA

Land titles are checked how far back into the past?

Titles are researched 60 years into the past.

Who can perform a real estate closing?

Closings are conducted by attorneys and lenders.

Who can prepare real estate closing documents?

Closing documents are prepared by attorneys and lenders.

How can a title be conveyed?

Title is conveyed through warranty deed. Title can be transferred through each of the common law conveyances. They are joint tenancy, tenancy in common, and tenancy by the entirety. Titles can be held as community property. Married people may hold titles as sole and separate property without consent of spouses. Spousal rights are not assumed. West Virginia recognizes adverse possession after 10 years.

What are the documentary or transfer taxes and fees?

Transfer taxes are charged in the form of deed stamps. The cost is $4.40 for each $1,000. The recording fee is independently set by each county.

Are closing costs open to negotiation?

The closing fees are negotiable.

What are the mortgage taxes?

Mortgage taxes are not levied in this state.

How is the mortgage secured?

Mortgage is secured through a deed of trust.

Is there a redemption period after the sale?

No.

How is a mortgage lien cancelled?

Mortgage liens are cancelled through a release.

For how long are judgment liens in effect?

Judgment liens are effective for 10 years.

Can property taxes be paid in installments?

Taxes are levied on July 1 and are due on September 1. They can be paid in semiannual installments due in September and March.

Is this a community property state?

No.

Are title insurance agents regulated?

Agents must be licensed by the Insurance Commissioner. Their rates are not regulated and can be negotiated.

What is the foreclosure process?

The process is usually carried out by the lender without the permission or oversight of a court. However, foreclosure can be through court order. The process must take a minimum of 30 days. West Virginia does not provide a redemption period.

Who pays closing costs?

Closing fees are negotiable.

Who handles consumer complaints?

1) Division of Banking, 304-558-2294, **www.wvdob.org/**.
2) Insurance Commission, 304-558-3354, **www.state.wv.us/insurance**. 3) Real Estate Commission, 304-558-3555, **www.state.wv.us/wvrec**.

Section 8.50: WISCONSIN

Land titles are checked how far back into the past?

Titles are researched 60 years into the past.

Who can perform a real estate closing?

Title companies, lenders, attorneys, and real estate agents.

Who can prepare real estate closing documents?

Closing documents are prepared by an attorney.

How can a title be conveyed?

Title is conveyed through a deed or mortgage. Title can be transferred through each of the common law conveyances. They are joint tenancy, tenancy in common, and tenancy by the entirety. Titles can be held as community property. Married people may hold titles as sole and separate property but only with consent of spouses. Spousal rights are assumed. Wisconsin recognizes adverse possession after 20 years.

What are the documentary or transfer taxes and fees?

Transfer tax is $.30 for each $100. The recording fee is $11 for the first page and $2 for each additional page.

Are closing costs open to negotiation?

The precedent is for the seller to pay the closing fees. The buyer pays the loan closing fees.

What are the mortgage taxes?

Mortgage taxes are not levied in this state.

How is the mortgage secured?

Mortgages are secured through a promissory note.

Is there a redemption period after the sale?

No.

How is a mortgage lien cancelled?

Mortgage liens are cancelled through a satisfaction.

For how long are judgment liens in effect?

Judgment liens are effective for 10 years.

Can property taxes be paid in installments?

Taxes are assessed and levied by December 15 and due before January 15. They can be paid in two installments that are due by January 31 and July 31. Interest is not applied to the installments, but 18 percent interest is added to late and delinquent payments.

Is this a community property state?

Yes.

Are title insurance agents regulated?

Agents and their fees are regulated with the insurance commission. However, the fees may be negotiated down.

What is the foreclosure process?

It is only conducted through court order. The minimum time required to process a foreclosure is determined by the flowing statute: Wis. Stat. Ann. § 849.01 *et seq.* (West 1994 & Supp. 1995). There is a two-month redemption period for abandoned properties. The redemption period for commercial real estate is three months and one to four months for residential property.

Who pays closing costs?

The precedent is for the seller to pay the closing fees. Buyers pay loan closing fees.

Who handles consumer complaints?

1) Department of Regulation and Licensing, Division of Enforcement, 608-266-2112, **www.drl.state.wi.us/**.   2)

Insurance Commission, 608-266-3585, TDD 1-800-947-3529, **www.oci.wi.gov/**.

Section 8.51: WYOMING

Land titles are checked how far back into the past?

Titles are researched back to their U. S. patent.

Who can perform a real estate closing?

Lenders, real estate agents, and title agents can perform closings.

Who can prepare real estate closing documents?

The closing documents can be prepared by lenders, real estate agents, and title agents.

How can a title be conveyed?

Title is conveyed through warranty deed or quit claim deed.

What are the documentary or transfer taxes and fees?

Wyoming does not levy a transfer tax. The recording fee is $6 for the first page and $2 for each additional page.

Are closing costs open to negotiation?

The precedent is for a 50-50 split.

What are the mortgage taxes?

Wyoming does not levy a mortgage tax.

How is the mortgage secured?

Mortgages are secured through the promissory note.

Is there a redemption period after the sale?

The redemption period varies from three months to one year depending on the size of the property. Lenders are given a 30-day redemption period.

How is a mortgage lien cancelled?

Mortgage liens are cancelled through a release.

For how long are judgment liens in effect?

Judgment liens are effective for 21 years but can be renewed.

Can property taxes be paid in installments?

Taxes are levied annually and are due on September 1 and March 1.

Is this a community property state?

No.

Are title insurance agents regulated?

Agents and their rates are regulated by the state Insurance Department.

What is the foreclosure process?

Foreclosure can be carried out by a lender or through a court. The minimum processing time varies by statute. The redemption period is either three months or one year. The creditor has a redemption period of 30 days.

Who pays closing costs?

The precedent is for a 50-50 split.

Who handles consumer complaints?

1) Department of Audit, Division of Banking, 307-777-7797, **www.audit.state.wy.us/banking.default.htm**. 2) Department of Insurance, 307-777-7401, **www.insurance.state.wy.us**. 3) Real Estate Commission, 307-777-7141, **www.realestate.state.wy.us/index. htm**.

Appendix

Agreement Making Property Community Property

Agreement is made this _____, 20___, between _____ and _____, husband and wife, residents of the county of _____, state of _____.

Recitals:

The parties are now married each to the other.

Husband is possessed of certain property which is in fact owned and held by him as his sole and separate estate.

It is the desire of husband to change and convert the legal status of the property from his sole and separate estate to the status of community property of himself and _____, his wife:

Therefore, in consideration of the premises and of the love and affection which husband has for his wife, it is agreed between the parties that all that certain property described in "schedule A" attached to and made a part of this agreement, is declared to be owned and held by the parties in community, in the same manner and to the same effect as if acquired by the parties during coverture from the joint earnings of these parties, as contemplated in section _____ of the _____ revised statutes of_____.

By Husband: _____

By Wife: _____

State of _____

County of_____

Sworn to and subscribed before me, a Notary Public, for the State of _____

_____County of _____This _____ day of _____ 20_____

By:_____Notary Public

My Commission Expires: This _____day of _____, 20 _____

ALTA Statement

ALTA LOAN AND EXTENDED COVERAGE OWNERS POLICY STATEMENT

Commitment No. _____

Loan No. _____

The undersigned certifies with respect to the land described in the above commitment:

1.   That, to the best knowledge and belief of the undersigned, no contracts for the furnishing of any labor or material to the land or the improvements on it, and no security agreements or leases in respect to any goods or chattels that have or are to become attached to the land to any improvement on it as fixtures, have been given or are outstanding that have not been fully performed and satisfied; that there are no unrecorded contracts to purchase the land; and that there are no unrecorded leases to which the land is subject, except as listed below, and that if any leases are listed below, they contain no options to purchase, rights of renewal, or other unusual provisions, except as noted here:

_____.

2.   That, in the event the undersigned is a mortgagor in a mortgage to be insured under a loan policy to be issued pursuant to the above commitment, the mortgage and the principal obligations it secures are good and valid and free from all defenses; that any person purchasing the mortgage and the obligation it secures, or otherwise acquiring any interest in it, may do so in reliance on the truth of the matters recited here. This certification is made for the purpose of better enabling the holds or holders, from time to time, of the above mortgage and obligations to sell, purchasers or pledge against any defenses to them by the mortgage or the mortgagor's heirs, personal representatives or assigns. Dated

_____

Signed by individual owner or seller _____

Signature of purchaser _____

The above statements are made by _____ not personally but as a trustee under the trust agreement known as Trust No. _____ and this date by virtue of the written authority and direction of the beneficiaries under the trust.

Dated _____.

Signed by trust officer or employee _____

Assignment of Contract

The undersigned Assignor, having executed a contract this _____day of _____
_____, 20_____.

between

By:_____

Contractor

and

By:_____

Contractee

concerning the property described as:

Street Address_____

Unit Number_____

City and State_____

Zip Code_____

hereby assigns all rights to said contract to:

By:_____

Assignee

in exchange for compensation in the amount of $_____._____

Assignee agrees to fulfill all terms, conditions, and contingencies of said Contract
and to perform as required in good faith and within any time periods established
by said Contract this _____day of _____, 20_____.

_____	_____
Assignor	Witness
_____	_____
Assignee	*Witness*

Assumption of Loan

Purchaser assumes and agrees to pay as part of the purchase price for the above described real property the balance owing upon the note evidencing a _____[e.g., FHA] insured loan described above. Purchaser agrees to pay the note according to its face and tenor, and to comply with the terms, obligations and conditions of the deed of trust and the rules and regulations of mortgagee and _____[e.g., Federal Housing Administration]. Purchaser agrees to pay to seller the balance of the purchase price above the_____[e.g., FHA] loan, in monthly installments in the amount above stated, including interest at the rate of _____% computed monthly.

Purchaser shall pay the total monthly payment at the office of the seller in _____ ____, and out of the total payment seller shall pay to the mortgagee the payments upon the _____[e.g., FHA] loan. When seller shall have been paid the amount due seller above the _____ loan, purchaser shall pay direct to the insured mortgagee.

Purchaser will apply to the above named mortgagee and _____ [e.g., Federal Housing Administration] to be accepted as an insured mortgagor or borrower on the above mentioned _____ [e.g., FHA] loan in place of the seller, when seller shall have been paid the balance of the purchase price above the _____ loan.

Seller agrees, when the full balance of the purchase price, above the _____ loan, together with all interest on it, has been paid by purchaser and purchaser has been accepted in place of the seller as an insured borrower, to execute and deliver to purchaser a good and sufficient warranty deed conveying the above described real property to the purchaser, in which deed the balance then owing upon the above mentioned _____ loan shall be assumed. Purchaser agrees to execute, acknowledge and deliver to the above mentioned mortgagee an agreement of assumption and release, assuming and agreeing to pay the above mentioned ____ _____ loan, and seller is released from any further liability on the loan.

By: _____
Buyer

By _____:_____
Seller

State of _____

County of_____

Sworn to and subscribed before me, a Notary Public, for the State of _____ _____County of _____

This _____ day of _____ 20_____

By:_____

Notary Public

My Commission Expires: This _____day of _____, 20 _____

Contract in Form of Earnest Money or Deposit Receipt— Seller's Receipt

This _____ day of _____ 20_____

Received of _____ $_____ as earnest money, and in part payment for the purchase of the following described property situated in the County of _____ and State of _____: _____, which we have this day sold and agreed to convey to _____ for $_____ on terms as follows: _____.

Complete abstract of title continued to date is to be furnished to purchaser at the expense of seller, after which _____ days is to be allowed purchaser for examination of title. If title to the premises is not good and cannot be made good within _____ days from date this date, this agreement shall be void and the above $_____ refunded. But if the title to the premises is now good, in the name of seller, or is made good in him within_____ days, and the purchaser refuses to accept the same, the $_____ shall be forfeited to _____. But this forfeiture shall in no way affect the right of either party to enforce the specific performance of this contract.

Signature of seller_____

I hereby agree to purchase the property for the price and upon the terms above mentioned, and also agree to the conditions of forfeiture and all other conditions expressed.

Signature of purchaser_____

Due-On-Sale Acknowledgement

WHEREAS,_____ _____

as Seller and _____ as

Purchaser have entered in to a certain purchase and sales agreement even date herewith, the parties fully understand, acknowledge an agree as follows:

1. Both Seller and Purchaser are fully aware that the mortgage(s) deeds of trust securing the property located at _____ contain(s) provisions prohibiting the transfer of any interest in the property without satisfying the principal balance remaining on the underlying loans and/or obtaining the lender's prior written consent (i.e., a "due-on-sale" clause), and that this transaction may violate said mortgage. Seller specifically understands that this completely at this time, and that this loan will remain in Seller's name and may continue to appear on Seller's credit report.

2. Seller and Purchaser execute this disclosure form after having had the opportunity to seek legal counsel as to the legal and financial implications of due-on-sale clause. The parties agree and understand that if said due on sale clause is enforced by the holders of said mortgages, the entire balance due under said mortgage/deeds of trust will have to be paid off. In this event, Seller and Purchaser agree to take all reasonable steps to satisfy said lender, including both parties taking steps to obtain financing and/or Purchaser submitting an application to formally assume liability for said obligations. Purchaser understands that in the event that the underlying debt is not paid off, the lender holding the deeds of trust may foreclose the property which will extinguish Purchaser's interest under the Installment Land Contract.

3. Seller and Purchaser hereby agreed to defend, indemnify and hold all parties involved in this transaction harmless from any liability in the event that the holders of the mortgages and/or deeds of trust on the aforementioned property are called due and payable.

By   Seller:_____

By Purchaser:_____

State of _____

County of_____

Sworn to and subscribed before me, a Notary Public, for the State of _____

_____County of _____

This _____ day of _____ 20_____

By:_____

Notary Public

My Commission Expires: This _____day of _____, 20 _____

General Warranty Deed

For good consideration, we_____ of _____, County of _____ State of _____, hereby bargain, deed and convey to _____ of _____ County of_____, State of_____, the following described land in _____county, free and clear with WARRANTY COVENANTS; to wit:

Grantor, for itself and its heirs, hereby covenants with Grantee, its heirs, and assigns, that Grantor is lawfully seized in fee simple of the above-described premises; that it has a good right to convey; that the premises are free from all encumbrances; that Grantor and its heirs, and all persons acquiring any interest in the property granted, through or for Grantor, will, on demand of Grantee, or its heirs or assigns, and at the expense of Grantee, its heirs or assigns, execute an instrument necessary for the further assurance of the title to the premises that may be reasonably required; and that Grantor and its heirs will forever warrant and defend all of the property so granted to Grantee, its heirs, against every person lawfully claiming the same or any part thereof.

Being the same property conveyed to the Grantors by deed of _____ _____, dated _____20___

WITNESS the hands and seal of said Grantors this____day of_____, 20____.

_____

Grantor

_____

Grantee

STATE OF _____ COUNTY OF _____

On _____before me, _____

personally appeared_____,
personally known to me (or proved to me on the basis of satisfactory evidence) to be the person(s) whose name(s) is/are subscribed to the within instrument and acknowledged to me that he or she/they executed the same in his/her/their authorized capacity(ies), and that by his/her/their signature(s) on the instrument the person(s), or the entity upon behalf of which the person(s) acted, executed the instrument.

WITNESS my hand and official seal.

Signature_____

Affiant _____Known _____Unknown ID Produced_____

Limited Real Estate Power of Attorney

We _____ do
hereby certify that I/We am/are the buyer(s) of the property located at:

_____.

And I/We, hereby authorize_____ to act on my/our behalf at the closing of the above real estate and to sign any and all necessary documents at said closing on my/our behalf.

By: _____
Buyer

By: _____
Buyer

State of _____

County of_____

Sworn to and subscribed before me, a Notary Public, for the State of _____
_____County of _____

This _____ day of _____ 20____

By: _____
Notary Public

My Commission Expires: This _____day of _____, 20 ____

Agreement to Purchase

This is a legally binding contract. If you do not understand this contract, please seek legal council. THIS AGREEMENT entered into on the _____ day of _____, 20__ by and between,_____ or his/her/their assignee(s), hereinafter referred to as "Buyer", and _____ _____, Hereinafter referred to as "Seller".

(1)   PROPERTY PURCHASED: In consideration of the mutual promises herein contained, the Seller agrees to sell, and the Buyer agrees to buy, in accordance with the terms and conditions of this Agreement, the following described Real Property, Situated in the City of _____, the County of _____ and the State of _____, and described as follows_____ _____. Together with all the improvements thereon, all privileges, appurtenances, easements, and all fixtures presently situated in said building, including, but not by way of limitation: all heating and air conditioning equipment including window units; all electrical, plumbing and bathroom fixtures; water softeners; shades; Venetian blinds; awnings; curtains, draperies, & traverse rods; storm windows & doors; window & door screens; affixed mirrors; wall to wall, stair, and similar attached floor covering and carpets; television aerials, and rotor operating boxes; garage door openers and similar operating devices; ranges, ovens, refrigerators, dishwashers, garbage disposal, trash compactors, humidifiers; washing machines; dryer; all affixed or built-in furniture and fixtures; all landscaping, trees and shrubs; all utility/storage buildings or sheds; all building and yard maintenance equipment and tools; all furniture and equipment used by or rented to the tenants; except:_____ _____. In addition to the above the following shall be included in the sale_____.

(2)   PRICE AND TERMS: Buyer hereby agrees to pay for said property the sum _____ Dollars ($_____) payable as follows:

(A)   personal note in the amount of _____ Dollars ($_____ _____) is attached hereto as "Earnest Money" to apply toward the purchase price. In the event the offer is not accepted or if Seller defaults in the performance of this contract or if Buyer terminates this contract as hereafter provided, the Earnest Money shall be promptly returned to Buyer.

(B)   The Buyer agrees to pay _____ Dollars ($_____ _____) as the down payment on the property From this down payment shall be subtracted the Earnest Money previously paid, and the amount required for repairs agreed to be done by Seller.

(C)   In addition, the Buyer shall deposit monthly with an escrow agent designated by the Buyer the amount necessary to make the payments to the following mortgage and lien holders and none others. Included is the mortgage to the Seller:

(3)   EVIDENCE OF TITLE: in the form of a title search and owner's policy of title insurance, will be furnished by Seller, and shall be subject to the approval of the Buyer. A preliminary binder shall be provided to Buyer, for his review and approval, 48 hours prior to closing.

(4)   SELLER'S CERTIFICATION: Seller certifies to Buyer that, to the best of Seller's knowledge (a) there is no termite damage to the REAL ESTATE; (b) the fireplaces, chimneys, electrical, plumbing, heating, air conditioning equipment and systems, and other items included herein will be operational on Possession; (c) the REAL ESTATE is zoned _____; (d) there are no pending orders or ordinances or resolutions that have been enacted authorizing work or improvements for which the REAL ESTATE may be assessed; and (e) no City, County or State orders have been served upon him requiring work to be done or improvements to be made which have not been performed.

(5)   INSPECTION: Seller agrees to give Buyer, and/or his agent, access to property prior to closing to inspect the entire premises. Inspection shall include every room, the roof, plumbing, wiring, structure, foundation and all mechanical components. Should any deficiencies be found, the Seller shall have the option of either repairing the deficiency, deducting the cost of the repair from the down payment, or notifying the Buyer that the Seller cannot meet the terms of this contract and refunding the Earnest Money deposited by the Buyer. Before closing the Seller shall furnish and pay for: (a) an inspection by a licensed exterminator stating premises to be free of infestation or damage by wood destroying insects (infestation and resulting structural damage shall be treated and repaired at Seller's expense)

(6)   CONVEYANCE AND CLOSING: Within _____ days from acceptance, or upon repair of any deficiency in building condition by Seller, as provided above, or within 5 days of receipt of assumption materials from seller's lending institution by closing agent, whichever is later, both parties shall deposit with the authorized escrow holder, selected by the Buyer, all funds and instruments necessary to complete the sale in accordance with the terms hereof. Seller shall be responsible for transfer taxes, deed(s) preparation; and shall convey marketable title to the REAL ESTATE by deed of general warranty in fee simple absolute, with release of dower, on or before _____, or at such sooner time as mutually agreeable to the parties hereto, free, clear and

unencumbered as of Closing, except restrictions and easements of record which do not adversely affect the use of the REAL ESTATE, except _____ and except the following assessments (certified or otherwise) Seller shall have the right to remove any and all encumbrances or liens at the Closing out of the Purchase Price. Possession shall be given subject to tenants' rights on or before _____ 20____.

(7)　　PRORATIONS: There shall be prorated between Seller and Buyer as of Closing all (a) real estate taxes and installments of assessments as shown on the latest available tax duplicate; (b) interest on encumbrances assumed by Buyer and (c) rents and operating expenses; with Buyer assuming liability for such items following Closing. Security and/or damage deposits, advance rentals or considerations involving future lease credits held by Seller shall be transferred to Buyer at Closing without proration.

(8)　　CONDITION OF IMPROVEMENTS: Seller agrees that on Possession, the REAL ESTATE shall be in the same condition as it is on the date of this Purchase Offer, except for ordinary wear and tear. In case the REAL ESTATE herein referred to is destroyed wholly or partially by fire or other casualty, Buyer shall have the option for 10 days thereafter of proceeding with the terms of this contract, with an agreed adjustment in the sale price, or of terminating this agreement and being repaid all amounts paid hereunder.

(9)　　DEFAULT: It is expressly agreed that upon the event of any default or failure on the part of the Buyer, to comply with the terms and conditions of this contract, that Seller agrees to accept the EARNEST MONEY deposit with payment of the personal note as full liquidated damages. Upon default by the Seller to perform under this agreement, all deposits and notes shall be returned to Buyer on demand, and Buyer shall not thereby waive any right or remedy he may have because of such refusal. Further, Buyer shall be reimbursed by the Seller for his reasonable expense of building inspection, credit report, and appraisal fees.

(10)　　SOLE CONTRACT: The parties agree that this Agreement to Purchase constitutes their entire agreement and that no oral or implied agreement exists. Any amendments to this Contract shall be made in writing, signed by all parties and copies shall be attached to all copies of the original Purchase Contract. The terms and conditions of this Contract are to apply to and bind and inure to the benefit of the heirs, executors, administrators, successors, and assigns of the respective parties. All provisions of this contract shall survive the closing. All parties are advised to seek competent advice, unless they fully understand all terms of the contract. Should there be any term or condition in this contract that is not in accord with the applicable legal statutes, either party may void that portion of the contract by having his lawyer furnish a written opinion stating the reason, and citing the proper law or court case.

(11)   LEAD WARNING STATEMENT: Every Buyer of any interest in residential real property on which a residential dwelling unit was built prior to 1978 is notified that such property may present exposure to lead from lead-based paint that may place young children at risk of developing lead poisoning. If the dwelling unit was built prior to 1978, Buyer has the right to inspect for lead, at Buyer's cost, for a minimum of ten (10) days following Contract acceptance.

(12)   EXPIRATION: This offer shall expire unless a copy hereof with Seller's written acceptance is delivered to Buyer or his Agent on or before _____
_____ (AM/PM/NOON/MIDNIGHT) on _____
20_____.

(13)   APPROVAL: The undersigned Buyer(s) has read, fully understands and approves the foregoing offer and acknowledges possession of a signed copy.

_____   _____
Witness   Buyer

_____   _____
Witness   Buyer

Date: _____ Time:_____   _____
                                                                  Buyer's Address:

ACCEPTANCE

The undersigned Seller(s) has read, fully understands and verifies the above information as being correct and accepts the foregoing offer; agreeing to sell the herein described property on the terms and conditions herein specified and acknowledges receipt of a signed copy.

_____   _____
Witness   Seller

_____   _____
Witness   Seller

Date: _____ Time:_____   _____
                                                                  Seller's Address

Works Consulted and Further Reading

Brenda J. Cunningham, *Tricks of the Trade: A Real Estate Broker's Inside Advice on Buying or Selling a Home,* Adams Media, Avon, Massachusetts, 2004.

Fredericksburg Titles, Inc. "What are Surveys?" 7/5/06, **http://www.fredericksburgtitles.com/surveys/**

Fred Ugast, "Sample Home Inspection Forms," 7/7/06, **http://www.hometechonline.com/bar-maint2/barroof.htm**, **http://www.hometechonline.com/bar-maint2/barheat.htm**, **http://www.hometechonline.com/bar-maint2/barstruc.htm**.

K.F. Boackle, *Real Estate Closing Deskbook,* 2nd ed., ABA Publishing, Chicago, 2003.

MaritalHome.com, "Real Estate Procedures Act (RESPA)," "3/9/06, **http://www.divorcenet.com/states/nationwide/real_estate_settlement_procedures_act**. 7/5/06.

Mary Hedley, "Tenant Estoppels," *Counsel to Counsel*, May 2004, **http://www.sheppardmullin.com,** viewed 7/5/06.

Northern California Home, " Home Buyer Checklist," **http://www.ncahome.com/HomeBuyerChecklist**, 7/7/06.

Northern California Home, "Six Week Moving Checklist," **http://www.ncahome.com/SixWeekMovingChecklist**, 7/7/06.

Northern California Home, "Staging Your Home Checklist," **http://www.ncahome.com/StagingList**, 7/7/06.

Northern California Home, "Title Insurance FAQs", **http://www.cahome.com/title_insurance_faqs1**, 7/7/06.

Robert Irwin, *Home Closing Checklist*, (New York: McGraw-Hill, 2004).

Roger Galor, 2004, **http://fountainoflaw.com**, 7/5/06.

Sandy Gadow, *Your Real Estate Closing: Answers To All Your Questions_ From Opening Escrow, To Negotiating Fees, To Signing Closing Papers*, (New York: McGraw-Hill, 2003).

Sharon Restrepo and Dwan Bent-Twyford, "Take Precaution When Buying A Tenant Occupied Property" 7/5/06, **http://gareia.org**, 2006.

Index